# The Musée d'Orsay

# The musée d'Orsay

Cover:
**Claude Monet
(1840-1926),
Blue Waterlilies,**
1916-19, oil on canvas,
200 × 200 cm.

1 **Claude Monet,
The Luncheon on the Grass,**
1865-66, oil on canvas,
248 × 217 cm.
This canvas only represents a section of what was an immense composition (approximately 4.60 m × 6m). Monet, who wanted to compete with the "great academic machines" in the Salon of 1866, spent a year on the work. He depicted the painters Courbet (to the left) and Bazille (in the center).

# Interview with Henri Loyrette, director of the Musée d'Orsay

2

2 **Paul Gauguin,**
***Self-Portrait***
***with Yellow Christ,***
1889-1890, oil on canvas,
38 x 46 cm.
This straightforward portrait
was purchased by Maurice Denis
the year Gauguin
died and hung in his dining room
alongside a self-portrait
by Van Gogh, the other heroic
figure of modern art.

**Beaux-Arts: The opening of the Musée d'Orsay
in 1986 was greeted with great enthusiasm
as well as controversy. The first results concerning
the public can be now be assessed.
Do you have the number of visitors you expected?**

Henri Loyrette: Yes. From the start,
the number of visitors far exceeded initial
estimates. In fact, this even created
some problems due to areas that were too
small and insufficient services.
As we had anticipated many more visitors
than at the Jeu de Paume,
we planned for 1.8 to 2 million visitors.
But the figure was actually much,
much higher. Initially, about 3 million people
visited annually: today, we have
from 2.5 to 3 million visitors per year.

**How does the public react to the architecture
and the museographic challenge,
both of which were hotly debated at the time?
Do these choices meet all
the museum's requirements?
Were there any necessary modifications?**

The "guest book" available for visitor
comments indicates that people
feel comfortable in the museum, even if they
do not always like the architecture.
They say that it's a pleasure to walk through
the museum, a pleasure to visit.
After ten years, Orsay has become a museum
accessible to everyone. Which was
not a forgone conclusion for a place that some
claimed was elitist by its very design.
There is a real intimacy between the public
and the space and collections.
It's a museum that has aged well. Overall, it is
the same as it was in 1986;
the materials used have stood up remarkably
well over time. If we have remodeled
some areas, it is only because no museum is
perfect from the start… Aside from
the rearrangement of certain collections due
to recent acquisitions, the main
modifications involved changing the colors of
some hanging spaces. The background

color in the Impressionist room was soon found to be too white, too harsh. We changed the color in 1994 for the Barnes Exhibition for a slightly tinted stucco, which is unanimously agreed to be infinitely better. We have also improved the lighting in many areas of the museum; this is a difficult problem in Orsay because the spaces are all very different. No two rooms are identical. Generally speaking, I believe it is important to plan improvements as extensions to the original 1986 design. Whether you like the museum or not, Orsay was a turning point in the history of museum construction, and in the history of architecture itself.

**How do you assess the acquisitions of this first decade? Which works do you consider to be the most remarkable?**

We have extremely important acquisitions in every field, although when discussing the most remarkable among them, paintings come to mind first, including Gauguin's *Self-Portrait with Yellow Christ*, which we purchased, or *The Origin of the World* by Courbet, which was donated, or *Starry Night* by Van Gogh, a gift (which demonstrates the range of our acquisition methods). And these are only our most recent acquisitions. We have also created a photographic collection and considerably expanded the department of decorative arts, which did not exist when the museum was created in 1978. We are constantly acquiring important work in all these areas. Among the most recent are a Van de Velde desk, a Barbedienne mirror and the donation of the Guimard collection. There are, of course, gaps in our collections that we must fill as soon as possible. This primarily concerns foreign artists: we have only a single Munch, one Klimt and two Burnes-Jones to represent the pre-Raphaelites.

Our first responsibility is to have a complete range in our strongest area, the Impressionists, but the price of these paintings is so high that our ambitions are severely curtailed.

**Is the Musée d'Orsay now considered to a model for other museums?**

The concept of the Musée d'Orsay was, and remains, unique. No other museum after Orsay has been devoted to a single period with a multi-disciplinary approach that includes literature and music along with the fine arts. To a certain extent no one has copied us, but Orsay has undoubtedly created another way of looking at the nineteenth century. Some foreign museums with French collections are starting to become interested, as we were the first to do, in areas other than Impressionism and post-Impressionism. The increasing interest in the late nineteenth century – the Symbolists and the Nabis – is due in part to Orsay.

**In your viewpoint, what is the greatest weakness of the Musée d'Orsay? And its greatest asset?**

Its weakness is linked to the building it occupies, in other words, a severe lack of space, which means that all the important works can not be exhibited, certain large paintings can not be hung, and the Art Deco collections can not be installed. Our acquisitions policy must take into account this handicap. Its asset it really the multi-disciplinary approach and a concentration on a given period, which is manifested on an architectural level by a compact, easily visited building. In an era of gigantic museums, with a multitude of departments, the coherence and compactness of the Musée d'Orsay are opportunities to be exploited.

**Interview by Pascale Bertrand**

# Art arrives at the station

*What a wonderful idea to house a museum dedicated to nineteenth-century art in a building constructed for the Universal Exposition of 1900! Yet the transformation from Victor Laloux's station to its inspired destiny as a museum did not occur smoothly – although even as a station, its admirers thought "it looked like a Palace of the Fine Arts." By Jean-Michel Charbonnier*

3 **Central aisle of the Musée d'Orsay.**

4 **Inside the Orsay station ca. 1900.**
© Roger-Viollet.
The sculpture gallery was installed just over the position of the tracks (in the foreground, the *Four Quarters of the World,* by J.-B. Carpeaux.

On May 24, 1871, in the thick of the bloody Commune, the Goncourt brothers discussed the Revolution in their Journal. "Over Paris floats a cloud of smoke, like the smoke that caps the smokestack of a gas plant. And all around us fall from the sky, like a black rain, small bits of burnt paper: the civil records and financial statements of France." A good share of this paperwork came from the Palais d'Orsay, headquarters of the Conseil d'Etat and the Cour des comptes, which was burnt down the previous day by the Communards, along with the nearby Hôtel de Salm and the Palais des Tuileries on the other side of the Seine. Twenty-five years later, the dark shell of the Palais d'Orsay was still standing. For a time, the political leaders of the Third Republic conceived of restoring the building to create a decorative arts museum. Indeed, in 1880,

5

Auguste Rodin received a commission for *The Gates of Hell* for this planned museum; the original plaster for this work is now actually in the Musée d'Orsay. The project was abandoned and the palace finally torn down to make room for the seventh and last large Parisian train station, constructed for the Universal Exposition of 1900. The Compagnie des chemin de fer d'Orléans finally won their case, arguing that the Austerlitz station was too remote from the city center. Three architects submitted projects: Lucien Magne, Emile Bénard and Victor Laloux, whose proposal was accepted in 1898.

Some people worried about constructing a "traveling factory" opposite the Tuileries, in one of the most aristocratic neighborhoods of the capital. Yet there was nothing to fear from the

monument built by Laloux (1850-1937), who had already designed a station, The Saint-Martin Basilica and the town hall for the city of Tours. The building was meant to look as little like an industrial site as possible: the metal structure was hidden under cut stone and a 370-room hotel was built to surround the station along the entire length of the rue de Bellechasse, the rue de Lille and part of the quay. The actual purpose of the station was indicated only by the existence of two large clocks, and by the statues representing Bordeaux, Nantes and Toulouse – three large towns along the railway route – as well as the face of Mercury, the god of travelers, perched on the top of a glass roof. The interior design was unusually luxurious, because Laloux was assured that smoke and steam would not damage it: the electric motor had been used for the first time in France on the Orsay-Austerlitz route. The architect, who had been awarded the Grand Prix de Rome, lined the main hall with a coffered ceiling, making it look like an ancient basilica.

After only two years of construction, the Orsay station was solemnly inaugurated on July 14, 1900. "I will be taken to the Quai d'Orsay at noon," enthused the painter Edouard Detaille that same year. "The station is superb and looks like a Palace of Fine Arts; and since the Palace of Fine Arts looks like a train station, I suggest to Laloux to exchange the two, if we still have the time." This enthusiasm crossed the Atlantic: the Orsay station was used as a model for Grand Central Station in New York and Union Station in Washington, among others. As the departure point for connections to southwest France, Orsay was an intensely active station for some 30 years. But with electrification, the trains became longer and the platforms at Orsay were too short to accommodate them. In 1939 the long-distance traffic stopped completely.

Abandoned by the SNCF (the French national train company), Orsay was used as a prison during the Liberation; a backdrop for several film, including one by Orson Welles, *The Trial* (1962), adapted from Kafka's novel; storage space for the Madeleine Renaud-Jean-Louis Barrault theater company; and was finally transformed into an auction house while the new

6

7

5 **The reception room of the former hotel in the station.**
© S. Couturier/Archipress.
"The station is superb and looks like a Palace of Fine Arts," admired the painter Edouard Detaille, commenting on the luxury of the decoration.

6 **Current view of the Musée d'Orsay from the right bank of the Seine.**
© J.-L.Bohin/Explorer.
The stone shells conceal the metal structures so well that it is impossible to immediately identify the essential function of the building.

7 **The Orléans station and the Quai d'Orsay at the turn of the century.**
© Roger-Viollet.
Starting from the historical heart of the city, the tracks of the "new Orléans station" ran along the Seine in the underground tunnel now used by the RER.

Hôtel Drouot was being built. The mentality of the 1960s was not particularly sensitive to nineteenth-century architecture and there was talk of tearing down the buildings to construct a conference center and large hotel. The model proposed by Guillaume Gilet and René Coulon was accepted just as a debate flared up over the destruction of the Halles building (designed by Baltard) across the river. With the increasing interest in nineteenth-century industrial architecture, the station and hotel were registered in the inventory of historical monuments, then acquired full status as classified buildings in 1978.

One year earlier, the president of the Republic, Valéry Giscard d'Estaing, decided to transform the site into a museum; in so doing, he confirmed the project proposed by Georges Pompidou and his Cultural Affairs Minister, Alain Duhamel, for a large museum project to create a link between the Louvre and the Beaubourg project. This museum, devoted to the second half of the nineteenth century and the early twentieth century, would finally provide a suitable home for the Impressionist paintings that were stacked in the Jeu de Paume, which had just received several donations (the Mollard collection and the Kaganovitch collection) and was too small. It would also house the post-Impressionist works in the Palais de Toyko and the Salon paintings confined in the storerooms of the Louvre and other national museums. This multidisciplinary museum would show all aspects of artistic creation: painting, sculpture and decorative arts, of course, but also photography, graphic arts, cinema, architecture and urbanism.

The competition, which involved six architectural firms, was won by the ACT firm, which consisted of Renaud Bardon, Pierre Colboc and Jean-Paul Philippon. Gae Aulenti joined the group in 1980 to take charge of the interior design, equipment and furnishings. Creating a large museum in a station "is a challenge because of the fundamental differences between the two buildings and their functions," wrote Jean Jenger in a monograph about Orsay (*De la gare au musée*, Electra-Moniteur, 1986). "Furthermore, to do this in a building classified as a historical monument is a total paradox." The rehabilitation of the buildings was executed with a remarkable integrity, as can be seen in the decors of the neo-Louis XV rooms and the dining room of the hotel; and in the new coffered staff ceiling in the main hall, molded over the old one to conceal the acoustic modules and air ducts.

Reflecting the pictorial abundance of the period from 1848 to 1870, the arrangement allows for a comparison of the various movements (realism, Ingres, history painting), while avoiding brutal confrontations. There is no promiscuity between the styles, no effort to create an atmosphere. The Impressionist and post-Impressionist paintings from the post-1870 period are exhibited on the top level, under a glass roof that provides overhead light. The middle level houses naturalism, symbolism and art nouveau. "Starting with the masterpieces is a required route," affirms Georges Duby. "It's not such a bad itinerary. Provided you never lose sight of what surrounds them, nor the obscure and productive diversity that lies below." And although Duby wrote these lines about a cathedral, they are equally true for stations, as is so well demonstrated by the Musée d'Orsay. **Jean-Michel Charbonnier**

**8 The great clock in
the central aisle, designed
by Victor Laloux.**
© S. Couturier/Archipress.
An example of the excessive
ornamentation represented
by the official style of the time,
the great clock, designed
by Victor Laloux, contrasts
with the functional sobriety of
the glass ceiling.

**9 Side view
of the central aisle.**
© S. Couturier/Archipress.
The staff coffers, exact
reproductions of the originals,
conceal the heating ducts
and the acoustic modules installed
to temper the noise
of the station (in the foreground,
Carpeaux's *Ugolin*).

**10 View of the main aisle.**
© S. Couturier/Archipress.
In the foreground, in front of one
of Gae Aulenti's "mastabas,"
three busts by Charles Cordier;
left, the plaster of *Imperial France
Protecting Agriculture
and Science* by J.-B. Carpeaux.

9

10

**11 Jean-Auguste-Dominique
Ingres (1780-1867),**
*The Spring,*
1856, oil on canvas,
163 x 80 cm.
It took Ingres 36 years – and the
help of two friends, painters
Desgoffes and Balze – to achieve
this ideal of chastity.

*12* **Gustave Courbet
(1819-77),**
*Origin of the World,*
1866, oil on canvas,
46 x 55 cm.
Until 1995, the burning realism of
this portrait was savored
behind closed doors: Khalil-bey,
who commissioned the
work, hid it behind a green veil,
then Jacques Lacan
covered it with a sliding painting
by Masson.

# 1848-1870 Conquering reality

*Although the academic system still reigned supreme, it was showing signs of wear in the years just before the War of 1870. Realism developed in opposition to history painting, which still held a place of honor in the Salon, until it was swept away by a deep desire for change and the scandal of the Salon des refusés of 1863. By Philippe Dufour*

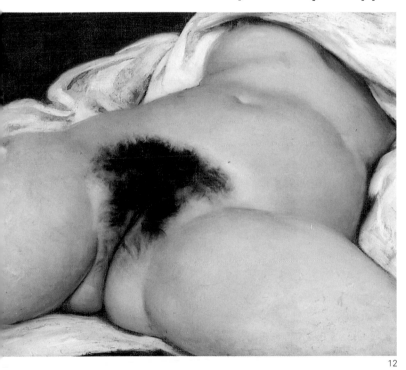

12

The Revolution of 1848 in Paris brought in its wake the short-lived Second Republic. But during the early months, Socialist and Republican ideology was the order of the day, especially in the arts. The provisional government let artists take part in their plans for a better society, in particular by organizing a competition for a symbolic representation of the Republic. Indeed, the modern concept of the ideologically committed artist may date from that time. The year 1848 constituted a turning point: a number of artists, seeing the profound changes taking place around them, refused the Romantic notion of art for art's sake and decided to take their subjects from life. The norms laid down by the Establishment, such as the Academy, were considered to be superfluous. As a symbol of this spirit and in the name of equality, the jury for the

1848 Salon was eliminated – which resulted in a show containing the best, but also the worst, works of art. Another sign of the times was the rise of a new school of painting at Barbizon and Chailly, two villages bordering the forest of Fontainebleau. Artists wanted to work in the open air, far from the iron rule of the Academy. The first artist to set up his easel there was Rousseau, followed soon after by Dupré, Daubigny, Troyon and Diaz de la Peña. They all wanted to break away from the official art world; implicit in their vision, which was basically that of the 1848 Revolution, that is, humanistic and slightly sentimental, was their need to work from nature. Their landscape paintings are in no way anecdotal; the only subject is the artist's emotions.

Corot was the first of these artist to paint directly from nature. The year 1850 corresponds to Corot's second style, as diffuse and misty as the light of the Ile-de-France region. Contrary to the Barbizon painters, he moved away from Realism, and his subsequent landscapes evoked a silent, unreal world.

The humanist spirit of 1848 is most apparent in the work of Jean-François Millet. He initially went to Barbizon to flee a cholera epidemic in

14

13

13 **Jean-Léon Gérôme
(1824-1904),**
*Cockfight,*
1846, oil on canvas, 143 x 204 cm.
"The young Greeks are in
marble, the cocks in
flesh and blood," exclaimed
Champfleury, referring to the
smooth, Ingres-like
modeling of these bodies.

14 **Jean-Auguste-Dominique
Ingres (1780-1867),**
*The Virgin of the Host,*
1854, oil on canvas,
113 x 113 cm.
A solitary genius of line and
form, Ingres claimed that
"drawing is the probity of art."
Although he never really
taught, many great artists, from
Degas to Picasso,
acknowledged his influence.

15 **Théodore Chassériau
(1819-56),**
*Tepidarium,*
1853, oil on canvas, 171 x 258 cm.
In a scene inspired from
the *Baths of Venus,* which had
recently been discovered
in Pompeii, Chassériau reconciles
his admiration for his master,
Ingres, and for Delacroix, in his
attention to both line and color.

Paris but ended up living there permanently. Himself the son of peasants, Millet was originally a portrait-painter, but in Barbizon began to depict the peasants around him. He portrayed them as if they were molded from the same earth they labored on. In his paintings, Millet gives them an timeless, noble quality, and their austere way of life, on the brink of dire poverty, is rendered in dull, earthy tones. Like the people he painted, Millet – misunderstood as a painter – had a difficult life. Recognition was posthumous, as *Gleaners* (17) and *The Angelus* (1857-1859) became world famous only after his death.

The manifesto of Realist painting was Gustave Courbet's *Burial at Ornans* (30), in which the artist used a format usually reserved for historical subjects to render a scene from village life. During the 1855 Universal Exposition in Paris, he clearly affirmed the existence of a new trend in painting by calling the wooden building where he was showing 40 of his canvases, including the important *Studio* (28), as the "Pavilion of Realism." It is true that many of his landscapes, nudes, portraits and still-life paintings are bathed in a peaceful, realistic atmosphere, but his large compositions, peopled with strangely silent figures, are more dreamlike than real.

The other outstanding representative of Realism was Honoré Daumier. A late-comer to painting, his beginnings as a cartoonist taught him to strip off the masks people try to hide behind, and his talents as a sculptor can be seen in the powerful, expressionistic rendering of his figures. Though there are still some Romantic themes in Daumier's subject matter, his work as a whole is marked by Realism, and figures like *The Laundress* (34) capture the universal qualities of ordinary people. Realism also had its official version; these works were accepted in the Salons and even awarded prizes. Jules Breton's *Calling the Gleaners Home* (1859) or Rosa Bonheur's *Ploughing in the Nivernais Region* (16), with their anecdotal, bucolic qualities, were still most welcome, unlike Courbet's or Millet's stark representations.

While Realism was controversial and divided into different movements, the leading lights of the artistic scene continued to be Ingres and Delacroix, who belonged to the preceding generation. Ingres succumbed once last time to his passion for the female body with *The Spring* (11), while Delacroix once again evoked his memories of North Africa with *The Tiger Hunt* (33) or

17

undertook outsized mural paintings like *Jacob Struggling With the Angel* (1856-1861), in the Church of Saint-Sulpice. The enormously successful retrospectives devoted to their works at the 1855 Universal Exposition consecrated them as major painters.

Yet this is not surprising: historical and mythological paintings still took pride of place, and reflected the tastes of the public that frequented the Salons. Indeed, the situation had scarcely changed since the previous century when commissions and recognition were given primarily to artists who did such "genre" works. The proper career for painters much younger than Ingres and Delacroix – such as Cabanel, Bouguereau, Henner or Regnault – was first to win a Prix de Rome, which entitled them to sojourn at the Villa Medici in Rome, then become a professor at the School of Fine Arts in Paris and finally win a seat at the Academy. Subject matter was taken

18

19 **Henri Fantin-Latour
(1836-1904),**
*A Studio in Les Batignolles,*
1870, oil on canvas,
204 x 273.5 cm.
A group of friends gathers
around the master in
Manet's studio: painters Renoir,
Bazille, Monet and Scholderer;
writers Astruc and Zola;
and musician and art collector
Edmond Maître.
(left to right : Scholderer, Manet,
Renoir, Astruc, Zola,
Edmond Maître, Bazille, Monet).

20 **Edouard Manet
(1832-83),**
*The Fife-Player,*
1866, oil on canvas,
161 x 97 cm.
This figure, which stands out from
a flat, single-colored background,
was painted on his return
from a trip to Spain and reflects
the influence of Velasquez.

21 **Ernest Meissonier
(1815-91),**
*The Campaign of France, 1814,*
1864, oil on canvas,
51.5 x 76.5 cm.
Meissonier ignored the lustre of
the uniforms in this
work, concentrating instead
on the bleak line of generals who
would all soon be traitors,
with the exception of one, Ney,
the real hero of this composition.

from ancient Greek and Roman mythology, from the Bible, or from ancient, modern and contemporary history. Technically, these painters were irreproachable, if not virtuosos; their brushstrokes recalled those of the old Venetian or Spanish masters, which justified their fame and their high prices. Later dubbed *pompiers* (as in "pomp" as well as "pompous"), these painters were an eclectic bunch, ranging from the brilliant Romantic painter Thomas Couture to the meticulous William Bouguereau.

The world of mythology and allegory was also a pretext for new pictorial research, which gave greater emphasis to the artist's emotional life. Gustave Moreau, who by the 1850s was extremely successful in the Salons, exhibited paintings with even more romantic coloring, but with a more precise and precious technique. His *Orpheus* (126) illustrates his favorite theme: the man/woman duality, or rather the clash of the male principle with the eternal feminine. Puvis de Chavannes also used allegory and idealization. As opposed to Moreau, his works aimed toward simplification; it was the unique timelessness of his paintings that stuck his

contemporaries. These two artists prepared the way for Symbolism, and they both became leading figures in this movement.

By the early 1860s, the situation was apparently stable but in the space of just a few years, a group of young painters broke the traditional boundaries of painting to invent modern art.
A leader in this adventure was Edouard Manet, who came from a wealthy family. He studied painting in Couture's studio, but he developed his own distinctive style of juxtaposing colors with very few gradations by copying paintings in the Louvre by Frans Hals and Velasquez. In 1863 he presented a large canvas at the Salon des refusés, established by Napoléon III for those who were turned away from the official Salon. The canvas in question, originally entitled *The Bath* and later renamed *Luncheon on the Grass* (40), created a furor. Two years later, his *Olympia* (41) was accepted at the Salon, but it, too, proved disturbing to the public. The Second Empire public saw only obscenity in Manet's works. People were incapable of seeing the similarity in subject matter and sumptuous technique between his canvases and those of such recognized masters

of the past as Giorgione, Raphael, Velasquez and Goya. Manet's choice of contemporary subjects was in fact merely a pretext to paint, but in doing so, he broke with the anecdotal tradition of his immediate predecessors. What he also did was to open the way for modern painting. By dint of scandal, Manet became famous, and was soon the head of a group of young painters that included Renoir, Monet, Sisley and Bazille, who had been working at Gleyre's studio since 1862 and who were all looking for a new way to go beyond the boundaries of academic painting. As can be seen in a later painting by Fantin-Latour, called *The Studio in Les Batignolles* (19), the young painters gathered around Manet in his studio or in a nearby café called the Café Guerbois, also frequented by Pissarro, Degas and Cézanne.

Edgar Degas, a contemporary of Manet and like him, from a well-to-do family, developed his own

personal style by studying and copying past masters, both in Paris and in Italy. His first works show he was familiar with such portrait painters of the Renaissance as Holbein and Clouet – as can be seen in *The Bellelli Family* (45) – or the fresco-painters of the Quattrocento, as in *Semiramis Overseeing the Construction of Babylon* (1861). But he was quick to pick up the discoveries of his time, learning lessons in cropping from photography and asymmetrical composition from Japanese prints, which he put to use in canvases with contemporary subject matter, as in *The Orchestra at the Opera* (70).

During the 1860s, one of the most pressing problems for the younger generation was how to render natural light and figures in nature. Degas did a series at the race track (*Racehorses in Front of the Grandstands*, 69). Following in the footsteps of Boudin and Jongkind, who experimented with light at the beaches and ports of Normandy a few years earlier, Renoir, Bazille, Monet and Sisley also used the gains made by realist painters like Courbet and the Barbizon School. Monet and Bazille rented lodgings at Chailly on the edge of Fontainebleau forest and were the first to paint out-of-doors. In 1865-66, Monet

22

**24 Claude Monet
(1840-1926),
*The Magpie,***
1868-69, oil on canvas,
89 × 130 cm.
Monet, who painted
the constanting changing effects
of light, demonstrated his skill at
rendering his subjects in this
fleecy snow-covered landscape
illuminated by the slanting
sunrays of a January afternoon.

24

23

25

created his own *Luncheon on the Grass* (1); its natural lighting stood in contrast to the abstract light of Manet's work. In 1867 the jury of the Salon refused his *Women in the Garden* (55); that same year, Bazille painted *Family Reunion* (26), in which he, too, tried to solve the problems posed by light and shadow. The experiments with outdoor light done by Monet in 1869 marks the birth of new kind of painting: like the canvases done by Renoir during the summer at La Grenouillère, on the banks of the Seine, Monet's *Magpie* (24), with its blue-tinged snow, announces the coming of Impressionism.

Modern trends had more difficulty coming to the fore in sculpture. Form remained solidly anchored in the past, and neo-classical works

26

continued throughout the century. Leading this field was James Pradier and a group of elegant sculptors known as the "Florentins," because they took their inspiration from the Italian Renaissance; the group included Mercier, Falguière and Moulin. A few sculptors struck out in other directions: among the Romantics were Rude, Préault and Barye; the few Realists included Daumier and Meissonier; and above all, Jean-Baptiste Carpeaux, a singular genius who drew his inspiration from the Renaissance and 18th-century French art to sculpt the figures of *The Dance* for the facade of the new Paris Opera house. Carpeaux succeeded in creating sculpture that was at once personal, vital and sensuous.

**Philippe Dufour**

25 **Edouard Manet (1832-83),**
*The Balcony,*
Salon of 1869, oil on canvas,
170 × 124.5 cm.
Inspired by Goya's *Manolas at the Balcony*, Manet represented in the foreground his future sister-in-law, the painter Berthe Morisot, who participated in the Impressionist exhibitions.

26 **Frédéric Bazille (1841-70),**
*Family Reunion,*
1867, oil on canvas,
152 × 230 cm.
The steady gaze and position of each figure within the group, posed on the terrace of the family home, imbues this reunion with a feeling of eternity.

27 **Frédéric Bazille**
*Bazille's studio,*
1870, oil on canvas,
98 × 128.5 cm.
Bazille painted his closest friends in his studio: near the artist, Manet and Monet; at the piano, Edmond Maître; and on the staircase, Zola. *The Fisherman with a Net* and the unfinished *Toilette* hang on the walls.

27

# Courbet

28 **Gustave Courbet
(1819-77),**
*The Painter's Studio: Allegory,*
1855, oil on canvas,
361 x 598 cm.

29 **Gustave Courbet,**
*The Wave,*
1870, oil on canvas,
117 x 160.5 cm.

30 **Gustave Courbet,**
*Burial at Ornans,*
1849-50,
oil on canvas,
315 x 668 cm.

Admirers of Realism never forgave Courbet for painting *The Studio* after *The Burial at Ornans*. In *The Burial*, the artist postulated such basic principles as the veracity of the scene observed, as well as borrowings from folk art, to create a long, seemingly naive frieze of people from his native village. He portrayed them paying a last homage to death. But in *The Studio*, the painter combined autobiography and allegory. Courbet gravely offered up a hymn to painting: he made references to his masters Rembrandt and Velasquez and created virtuoso pieces. The artist's dream of reviving the art of his time was realized in the two paintings that now hang in the Musée d'Orsay. M. H.

29

28

30

# Orientalism

31

32

Ingres had merely dreamed of the Orient with his *Odalisques*, but the Romantics actually traveled there (Decamps left for Turkey in 1828 and Delacroix for North Africa in 1832). Colonial conquests coupled with the World Fairs had developed peoples' taste for exoticism, and more and more painters – both landscape artists and traditional academic painters – began to travel to the Orient. They avidly filled their sketchbooks with landscapes and scenes from daily life in the countries they visited. Most of them wanted to discover lifestyles that had not changed since biblical times or Antiquity. The Orient was also used as a pretext to depict imaginary or historical scenes strongly tinged with eroticism. P. D.

31 **Charles Vacher
de Tournemine
(1812-72),**
*Café in Adalia (Turkey),*
Salon of 1861,
oil on canvas, 69 x 124 cm.

32 **Henri Regnault
(1843-71),**
*Arbitrary Execution
Under the Moorish Kings of
Grenada,*
1870, oil on canvas,
302 x 146 cm.

33 **Eugène Delacroix
(1798-1863),**
*The Tiger Hunt,*
1854,
oil on canvas,
73.5 x 92.5 cm.

# Daumier

When Daumier painted, he gave free reign to a tenderness and simplicity that are absent in his stinging lithographs created for the press. His favorite subjects were street scenes, working people, popular entertainment, theater and circuses, as well as print collectors, one of his preferred themes. But the real masterpiece in the Daumier room of the Musée d'Orsay is the series of 36 busts of parliamentarians, sculpted on the request of Charles Philippon, editor-in-chief of *La Caricature*. These works ruthlessly depict the political class of the July Monarchy. "These busts are the sputtering embers of savagery, burning with passion," wrote a critic of the time. M. J.

34

34 **Honoré Daumier (1808-79),** *The Laundress,* ca. 1863, oil on wood, 49 × 33.5 cm.

35

36

# Salon painting

37 **Thomas Couture (1815-79),**
*Romans in the Period of Decadence,*
1847, oil on wood,
472 x 772 cm.

38 **Alexandre Cabanel (1823-89),**
*Birth of Venus,*
Salon of 1863,
oil on canvas, 130 x 225 cm.

39 **William Bouguereau, (1825-1905),**
*Birth of Venus,*
1879,
oil on canvas,
303 x 216 cm.

38

The 1848 Revolution constituted a rude awakening for a number of French artists, who suddenly became interested in their own period and realized that it was important to capture its myriad aspects in painting. But many others were content to continue to depict the gods and heroes that had been portrayed in art ever since the 15th century, a tradition that was to be perpetuated throughout the 19th century. These artists preferred to depict classical scenes, so as not to be excluded from the annual Salon. Moreover, the public was more readily attracted to subjects represented by works in the Louvre, rather than those they saw in the streets every day. Museum pieces thus remained the obligatory reference point for artists and collectors alike. P. D.

37

39

# Manet

In 1863, Cabanel's painting, *The Birth of Venus*, won unanimous praise from the jury of the official Salon and was bought by Napoleon III. That same jury refused 3,000 other works, which were all excluded from the official show. To give the public a chance to judge for themselves, the Emperor decided to set up the "Salon des Refusés," and it was there that Manet, already considered the head of the young school of painting, presented his *Luncheon on the Grass*. The public had never understood Manet's direct manner of handling modern subjects, but found this particular painting profoundly shocking. By deliberately refusing to depict historical fiction or idealize his subject, Manet forced his contemporaries to look at the world in a very different way. In 1865 he provoked

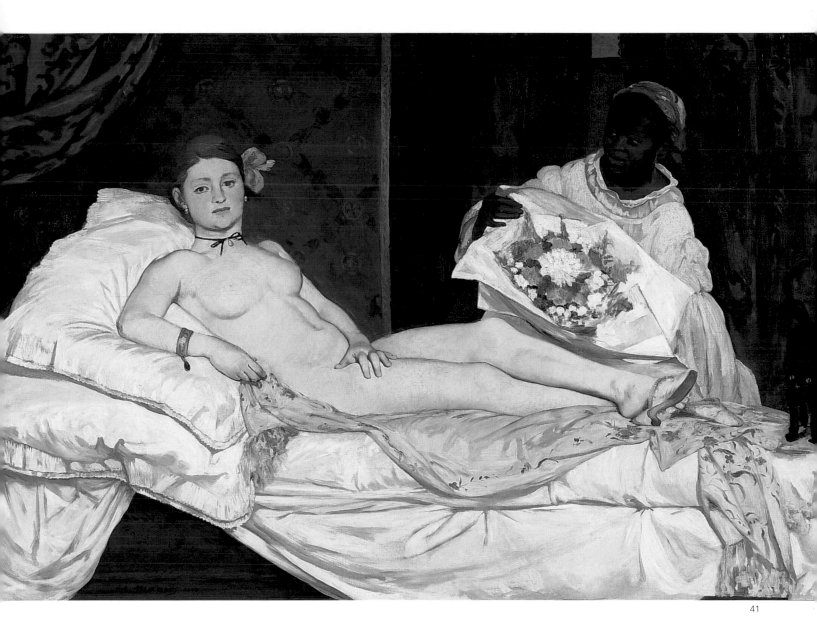

another scandal with his *Olympia*. What did the public at the Salon find most shocking about the work? Was it the direct cold rendering of the female body? And although the contrast is less strong today, was it the artist's technique of mixing bright colors with black? His simplification of forms? Or was it the rather prudish verses by Zacharie Astruc that accompanied the canvas, in which the poet referred to the courtesan as "an august young woman whose flame has been dampened?" P. D.

40 **Edouard Manet (1832-1883),** *Luncheon on the Grass,* 1863, oil on canvas, 208 × 264.5 cm.

41 **Edouard Manet,** *Olympia,* 1863, oil on canvas, 130.5 × 190 cm.

# Portraits

42

43

In the second half
of the nineteenth century,
portraiture was
still a predominant genre
favored by the
great masters. Although
Carolus-Duran
is a typical example of the
fashionable portraitist
adored by a
bourgeois clientele, many
other artists
preferred more intimate
portraits; they
painted their subjects
in familiar settings

and emphasized
the psychological aspects.
Indeed, Degas revealed
the dissension
reigning in the Bèllelli
family, while Whistler
expressed the
solitude of aging through
a stark composition and a
range of ash-gray
colors. The frequent use
of pure black
during this period can
be explained in part by
the rediscovery
of Spanish painting. M. J.

44

42 **Franz Xaver Winterhalter (1806-73),**
*Madame Rimsky-Korsakov,*
1864, oil on canvas,
117 × 90 cm.

43 **Charles Carolus-Duran (1837-1917),**
*Woman with a Glove,*
*Madame Carolus-Duran,*
1869, oil on canvas,
228 × 164 cm.

44 **James Whistler (1834-1903),**
*Artist's Mother,*
1871, oil on canvas,
144.3 × 162.5 cm.

45 **Edgar Degas (1834-1917),**
*The Bellelli Family,*
1858-1867,
oil on canvas,
200 × 250 cm.

45

# Carpeaux

46

47

48

46 **Jean-Baptiste Carpeaux
(1827-1875),**
*Four Quarters of the World,*
1872, plaster model,
280 x 177 x 145 cm.

47 **Jean-Baptiste Carpeaux,**
*The Dance,*
1868, plaster model
for the facade of the Paris Opera,
232 x 148 x 115 cm.

48 **Jean-Baptiste Carpeaux,**
*Eugénie Fiocre,*
1869, plaster bust,
83 x 51 x 37 cm.

49 **Jean-Baptiste Carpeaux,**
*Ugolin,*
1860, terra-cotta study,
56 x 41.5 x 28.4 cm.

**When Jean-Baptiste Carpeaux was studying in Rome at the Villa Medici, he was required to send a work to Paris every year. For one of these sculptures, he chose a modern subject inspired from Dante's** *Hell.* **He used the emblematic figure of** *Ugolin* **to express the suffering of the human condition, which was a radical break from the conformist academic style. When Carpeaux returned to Paris he began a career as an official illustrator/chronicler of the Imperial family.**

**He was a versatile artist: he not only designed large decorative groups commissioned by his patrons – including** *The Dance* **for the Garnier Opera and** *The Four Quarters of the World* **for the fountain in the Observatoire Gardens – he was also able to create more intimate scenes and portraits that revealed a sensitive psychological insight. Carpeaux's style of expressing movement, his vibrant rendering of skin and the realism of his figures made him one of the pioneers of modern sculpture. C. N.**

# 1874-1886
# The Impressionist adventure

*After the War of 1870, young avant-garde artists regrouped far from the influence of official institutions.*
*The first independent exhibition was held in 1874 by a group that became known as the Impressionists. Although they supported no particular aesthetic theory, they fought – in the midst of total incomprehension – for a new way of painting based on a new of seeing. By Caroline Larroche*

51

In the late 1860s, Manet, Renoir, Bazille, Pissarro and Sisley had still not fully realized where they were heading as they experimented with capturing light out of doors. In this respect, the Franco-Prussian War of 1870 had a decisive influence, for it forced these artists to go their separate ways. Renoir was called into the army, Cézanne moved to the south of France at l'Estaque, Bazille was killed at the front while Pissaro and Monet fled the war and poverty in France to take refuge in London, where they hoped to be able to work and sell their paintings. As Pissarro confided years later, "We also went to museums. Turner's and Constable's water-colors and paintings certainly influenced us… Their experiments with outdoor scenes, light, and fleeting effects were closer to our own preoccupations." This discovery precipitated

50 **Claude Monet**
**(1840-1926),**
***The Hotel des Roches Noires.***
***Trouville,***
1870, oil on canvas, 81 x 58.5 cm.
Trouville, a fashionable
seaside resort, attracted painters
both for its beauty
and as a place to meet patrons.
Monet stayed there in 1870
with his wife and newborn child.

51 **Edouard Manet**
**(1832-84),**
***On the Beach,***
1873, oil on canvas,
59.6 x 73.2 cm.
Manet concentrated
his attention on the two figures
(Mme Manet and his
brother Eugène) idling dreamily
on the beach, rather
than on the landscape itself.

**52 Camille Pissarro**
**(1830-1903),**
*Red roofs.*
*Village Corner, Winter,*
1877, oil on canvas,
54.5 x 65.5 cm.
Pissarro had a marked
preference for rural landscapes
and painted numerous views of
villages in Ile-de-France, such as
this work made when he lived in
Pontoise, from 1872 to 1882.

**53 Paul Cézanne**
**(1839-1906),**
*House of the Hanged Man,*
*Auvers-sur-Oise,*
1873, oil on canvas, 55 x 66 cm.
Painted in Auvers-sur-Oise while
Cézanne was staying with
Pissarro, this painting seems to
be inhabited by a hidden drama,
although it is unlikely there was
ever a hanged man in this house.

**54 Claude Monet**
**(1840-1926),**
*The Pavé de Chailly, Forest of*
*Fontainebleau,*
ca. 1865, oil on canvas,
43.5 x 59 cm.
The region of Chailly-en-Bière
was made famous by the
landscape painters of the Barbizon
school. Starting in 1863, Monet
and his friends frequently visited
the area to paint from nature.

**55 Claude Monet,**
*Women in the Garden,*
1867, oil on canvas,
255 x 205 cm.
This canvas may be the largest
painting ever made
in the open air. It reflects the
ambitions of Monet,
who wanted to give
this open-air painting the dignity
of a history painting.

54

52

53

their own artistic evolution. Rain, snow and fog became subjects of study that allowed them to go even further in their observation of light, the rendering of fleeting effects, and the division of color. It was also in London that they made a decisive encounter: Daubigny introduced them to the art dealer Durand-Ruel, the same man who had dared to defend Courbet and later Manet. Durand-Ruel took up the banner of this group of contested avant-garde artists, and never failed to give them his unwavering support. This was especially important as their paintings were systematically turned down by the increasingly adamant juries of the official Salons. This refusal led them to band together to defend their common goals.

Monet, Pissarro, Renoir, Berthe Morisot and Sisley, with the support of Degas, founded the "Limited Company of Painters, Sculptors and Engravers," which was set up to organize independent exhibitions without juries or prizes. Manet, who had been the unwilling spokesman for the group ever since the scandal of the 1863 Salon des Refusés, refused to join their company. The salon, he felt, was the "best place to join battle." The first show was held in 1874 in the studios of the photographer Nadar on the boulevard des Capucines, near the Opera. Thirty artists participated, among them Guillaumin and Cézanne (presented by Pissarro), De Nittis, Legros and Bracquemond (presented by Degas), Boudin and Jongkind, and 165 works were on view. Established art critics were more than ever convinced that these were absurd daubings, and railed against the painters "who

have declared war against beauty." Art critic Louis Leroy joined the chorus, mocking Monet's *Impression: Rising Sun* (Marmottan Museum, Paris). "Impression... I knew it must be something like that. As I'm impressed, there must be some impression somewhere... "

The term "Impressionism" became a catchword, and even the artists themselves adopted it, as did their small circle of friends, art critics and collectors (which included Jules Castagnary, Edmond Duranty, Théodore Duret and Georges Rivière). Over the next 12 years, until 1886, seven other exhibitions were organized under the Impressionist banner, and this in spite of bitter attacks from without and squabbling, both personal and aesthetic, from within. Some artists broke away: Cezanne after 1877, Monet, Sisley and Renoir in 1880 ind 1886. But new artists took their place: Gustave Caillebotte in 1876, Mary Cassatt and Gauguin in 1879, and Seurat and Signac in 1886. During the 1860s the group spent a good deal of time discussing what the term "impression" really involved, without, however, examining the distant sources – Delacroix, Watteau, Fragonard, Vélasquez and Goya – or even such immediate precursors as Corot and Courbet. "The meetings at the Café Guerbois," commented art critic Théodore Duret, "were very fruitful. Manet contributed his use of lighter colors to painting and Claude Monet, Pissaro and Renoir brought with them the techniques of painting out of doors. From these meetings developed the impressive development in art which became known as Impressionism."

56 **Alfred Sisley (1839-99),**
*Boat During the Flood,*
*Port-Marly,*
1876, oil on canvas,
50.5 × 61 cm.
This subject inspired Sisley
to paint seven canvases, which
are among his most famous
compositions. In this version,
the painter has ignored
the drama to concentrate on the
blue of the sky.

57 **Claude Monet**
**(1840-1926),**
*Study of a Figure in Nature,*
*Woman with*
*Umbrella Turned to the Left,*
1886, oil on canvas,
131 × 88 cm.
Monet made several decorative
panels, using Suzanne Hoschédé,
his second wife's daughter,
as a model. This was the last time
he represented the figure.

57

Though they had no aesthetic theory per se, these artists developed a new way of painting through a new way of looking at things, born of immediate sensations. Because the light changed constantly, what they saw also changed continually, and these "fleeting impressions" became the real subject of their paintings, forcing artists to abandon traditional principles. Perspective no longer obeyed the strict rules of geometry: it was defined instead by a division of colors, just as broken brushstrokes, rather than line, suggested form and volume. Applying the theories of Chevreul on the chromatic circle and optical mixing, the Impressionists used only primary colors (red, blue and yellow) and complementary colors (orange, violet and green). By juxtaposing them on their canvases, they wanted to render all the vibrating colors in the air. Their aim was to capture what they saw, encompassing both the realities of daily life and the ephemeral aspects of nature. A large number of canvases painted prior to 1872-74 reflect their common concerns and include similar kinds of pictoral experiments, particularly the canvases painted in 1869 by Monet and Renoir at La Grenouillère.

Monet's influence became so preponderant that he was soon looked upon as the leader of the group. On his return from England via Holland, Monet settled at Argenteuil in 1871, where he stayed until 1878. Despite serious financial

58

59

problems, he worked hard, more often than not using a boat set up as a studio, like Daubigny before him. Tirelessly he sought to capture the effects of light in the sky and on the water, the vibrations set in motion when the sun came out or when clouds turned the sky gray, as in the canvases of *Sailboats at Argenteuil* (67). Water fascinated him to such an extent that he once declared: "I would always like to be in it or on it, and when I die, I want to be buried in a life-preserver." Capturing successive instants of vision, Monet varied his technique by using broken brushstrokes of bright tones, dividing colors into their components, and breaking up surfaces and masses. The canvases painted during this period attest to Monet's exacerbated sensibility and to his growing ability to render fleeting light effects on the rippled surface of the water, including the unpredictable effects of the wind. Water was to be one of the major themes of the Impressionists, who came in

turn to work with Monet at Argenteuil. They compared notes as they painted side by side, measuring their audacity in using colors but keeping their own distinctive styles. Even Manet, who had kept his distance and had refused to participate in their group shows, turned up at Argenteuil during the summer of 1874. Working out of doors alongside his painter friends had a definite effect on his work, for from that point on, his paintings became much more luminous. Unlike Monet, who worked with broken brushstrokes of contrasting colors to meld together his figures and the surrounding air, Manet wanted to emphasize form, which he did by using more intense colors and Japanese-style asymmetrical composition. Caillebotte's early works, like *Planing the Floor* (77), were marked by Realism, but Monet's influence can be seen starting in the 1880s, when the artist devoted himself almost exclusively to painting the Seine.

58 **Alfred Sisley**
**(1839-99),**
*Snow at Louveciennes,*
1878, oil on canvas,
61 x 50.5 cm.
This theme is typical of the
research of the
Impressionists. Like Monet and
Pissarro, the English painter Sisley
used small brushstrokes
to describe the fleecy effect of
the snow.

59 **Berthe Morisot**
**(1841-95),**
*The Cradle,*
1872, oil on canvas, 56 x 46 cm.
Madame Pontillon
(maiden name Edma Morisot),
the artist's sister
and his daughter Blanche.
The sentimental nature
of this painting, which shows the
influence of her
brother-in-law and teacher,
Manet, made it one
of the rare works appreciated by
the public during
the first Impressionist exhibition.

60 **Edouard Manet**
**(1832-83),**
*Portrait of Madame Edouard*
*Manet on a Blue Sofa,*
ca. 1874, pastel, 49 x 60 cm.
The pose has an ironical
resemblance to *Olympia,* painted
some ten years earlier.
The meaning here, however,
is entirely different: Manet
skillfully used pastel to create a
scene of domestic harmony.

60

61

**Auguste Renoir
(1841-1919),**
61 *Dance in the Country,*
62 *Dance in the City,*
1883, oil on canvas,
180 × 90 cm.
Designed as a pair, these
works were almost
always shown together, starting
with the first exhibition in
1883 in the Durand-Ruel gallery.

Art critic Armand Silvestre was not far off the mark when he wrote in 1874 that "Monet is the cleverest and the most daring, Sisley the most harmonious and the most timid, and Pissarro the most realistic and the most naive." No doubt Sisley suffered even more than his friends from poverty and public incomprehension. His canvases reveal a quiet equilibrium born of delicate tones of gray, pink and light green. Typical works are *Boat During the Flood* (56), in which the sky, water and earth become one, and *Snow at Louveciennes* (58). As for Pissarro, in 1872 he moved to Pontoise, some 20 miles north of Paris, where he painted in the company of Cézanne. Though his harmony of colors and his light brushstrokes show incredible freedom, a strong, structured composition serves to anchor his works. Pissarro preferred small country villages to waterscapes. He was a true naturelover, and it was only poor health that forced him to leave the countryside for Paris, where he painted a number of cityscapes, years after Renoir and Monet.

The French capital was the crucible of modern life, and as early as 1872, both Monet and Renoir used it as the subject of some of their best works (Monet's *Rue Montorgueil Decked Out With Flags, June 30 1878*, 63). They succeeded in capturing its fast pace and its special light in dynamic and daring plunging views, as they looked down from the windows where they had set up their easels. Train stations were another emblem of the modern world that Monet, for one, wanted to capture. He was captivated by the rich possibilities of the subject, with forms that constantly changed because of the steam roiling around the engines. He did a total of seven paintings of the *Saint-Lazare Station* (65), the first of many series on a single subject.

Renoir applied the principles of Impressionism to his figure paintings and, as he excelled at portrait-painting, he made his livelihood from it. In 1876, Renoir painted three of his most famous canvases: *Dancing at the Moulin de la Galette* (68), a scene showing working-class couples dancing in a country setting; *The Swing* (81); and *Study. Torso, Effect of Sun* (80), which critics castigated as a "pile of decomposing flesh." All these works are animated by a play of pink light and blue shadows, which simultaneously hides and reveals forms as rays of sunlight dart through the leaves.

Though Degas was the main organizer of the Impressionist exhibitions, he joined up with these painters not out of common convictions but to defend artistic freedom, to gain recognition and to sell his work. "My art," he claimed, "is anything but spontaneous. What I do is the result of reflection and the study of the great masters." Rather than paint out of doors, Degas preferred "what one sees in one's memory." To Pissarro, he once explained, "You need natural life, whereas what I need is artificial life." Whether he worked in oils, watercolors or pastels, Degas chose decidedly contemporary subjects: the hubbub of the racetrack (as in *Racehorses in Front of the Grandstands*, 69); the magic of singers in popular cafés or dancers at the Opera (*The Star*, 74); café scenes (*Absinth*, 79); and lastly, portrayals of laundry-women and milliners. Each time, though, Degas chose to show not the glitter but the hard work behind the scenes. In each case, too, the artist chose to explore movement by breaking down gestures, to experiment with space by using asymmetrical composition and ingenious cropping, and to try new chromatic effects. In Degas's own words, he was "the classical painter of modern life." And by successfully coupling complete technical mastery with great freedom, his works recorded an instantaneous vision of an immediate reality.

62

During the "heroic" 1870s, the quality of the Impressionists' work was matched only by the disdain of the critics. But by the end of the decade, when the movement was getting a modicum of recognition, spontaneity was decidedly on the wane. Certain artists in the group, including Pissarro and Renoir, were becoming aware of the defects – and even the dangers – of the movement. By this time, these various artists who had come a long way together had reached a certain artistic maturity and decided to part company. Their experience as a group came to a definite end with an eighth and last exhibition, in 1886, which no longer went under the name of "Impressionism." Furthermore, some of the major figures did not participate in it: Monet, Sisley and Renoir were notable for their absence. What was left for these artists to share was the gradual recognition of art lovers and critics, and at long last, of the public at large. Meanwhile, a new aesthetic evolution began in the early 1880s with Seurat, Gauguin, Van Gogh and Toulouse-Lautrec. True, they had been nourished by Impressionism but they then took a stand against it.

**Caroline Larroche**

63

**63 Claude Monet**
**(1840-1926),**
*Rue Montorgueil*
*Decked Out with Flags,*
*June 30 1878, During*
*the Universal Exposition,*
1878, oil on canvas,
81 x 50.5 cm.
Monet translated the popular euphoria filling the gaily decorated street through
an exuberant display of color.
The vibrant brushstrokes almost transform the composition into an abstract work.

**64 Paul Cézanne**
**(1839-1906),**
*L'Estaque, View of the Bay of*
*Marseille,*
1878-1879, oil on canvas,
59.5 x 73 cm.
Cézanne painted landscapes by synthesizing the planes into colored masses. This abolition of traditional perspective far exceeded the ambitions of the Impressionists.

64

65 **Claude Monet,**
*Saint-Lazare Station,*
1877, oil on canvas,
75.5 x 104 cm.
Monet rented an apartment near
the station, where he
was allowed to paint. He made a
series of ten different views
of the station, eight of which
were shown in the Impressionist
exhibition of 1877.

65

# In the open air

66

67

"We enjoyed the day," wrote the Goncourt brothers in 1865, "the fatigue, the speed, the fresh air, the warm sun, its rays darting about on the land. We were drunk with a near-animal joy of being alive on a broad river in beautiful weather and blinding light." These lines illustrate the radiant vitality born of fresh air that the Impressionist painters tried to convey. Starting in the mid-19th century, the less-privileged classes from the capital liked to go up to the Moulin de la Galette in the nearby village of Montmartre, or to the banks of the Seine at Argenteuil, Bougival and Marly. There they would enjoy bathing, canoeing, dancing in inexpensive open-air restaurants or picnicking. C. L.

66 **Claude Monet (1840-1926),** *Poppies, near Argenteuil,* 1873, oil on canvas, 50 × 65 cm.

67 **Claude Monet,** *Sailboats at Argenteuil,* 1874, oil on canvas, 60 × 100 cm.

68 **Auguste Renoir
(1841-1919),**
*Dancing at the Moulin
de la Galette, Montmartre,*
1876, oil on canvas,
131 x 175 cm.

# Degas

69

70

71

69 **Edgar Degas
(1834-1917),**
*Racehorses
in Front of the Grandstands,*
ca. 1879,
oil on canvas, 46 × 61 cm.

70 **Edgar Degas,**
*The Orchestra at the Opera,*
1868-69, oil on canvas,
56.5 × 46 cm.
In the foreground, Désiré Dihau,
bassoonist for the Opera
Orchestra, a friend of Degas.

71 **Edgar Degas,**
*Young Dancer of Fourteen,*
1881, patined bronze,
cotton skirt, satin ribbon,
103.8 × 48.8 cm.

Degas was a contemporary and friend of the Impressionists, but he maintained a distance from their research, stating that "I am quickly overcome by boredom when contemplating nature." He preferred to track down contemporary life as a pitiless analyst, scrupulously observing the postures of dancers in tutus as well as horses at the racetrack.

He painted women without artifice, surprised in the intimacy of their daily lives. Degas was an ardent defender of realism and was influenced by both photography and Japanese art (particularly works by Hokusai), which contributed to his unusual compositions that combined elliptical shortcuts, close-ups and truncated figures.

The quality of his line owes much to Ingres, while the audacious colors were inspired by Veronese and Delacroix. He was equally skilled with oils, pastels and engraving techniques. He superimposed materials and tried new techniques; indeed, for Degas, "sculpture is an experience to be added to the others." C. N.

72

72 **Edgar Degas,**
*The Tub,*
1886, pastel, 60 × 83 cm.

# Theater and dance

73 **Edgar Degas (1834-1917),** *Dress Rehearsal for a Ballet,* 1874, oil on canvas, 65 × 81 cm.

74 **Edgar Degas,** *The Star or Dancer on Stage,* 1876-77, pastel on monotype, 60 × 44 cm.

75

73

74

A number of artists chose such typically modern subjects as the world of entertainment and, unlike the Impressionists who liked to paint out of doors, they studied the effects of artificial lighting. The elegant Edgar Degas was an ardent music lover who attended the Opera assiduously. He rendered the half-light of the orchestra pit and the spiraling light that seemed to sculpt the bodies of ballet dancers on stage, in the wings and during rehearsals. Henri de Toulouse-Lautrec, better than anyone, rendered the atmosphere of turn-of-the-century Paris music halls and their ephemeral stars. As a regular visitor to the Moulin Rouge, Rat-Mort, Chat Noir, Mirliton and Divan Japonais and others, Toulouse-Lautrec liked to paint the other customers with, according to Fénéon, a "ferocious and measured exaggeration." C. L.

75 **Henri de Toulouse-Lautrec (1864-1901),**
*Henry Samary,*
*from the Comédie-Française,*
1889, oil on cardboard,
75 × 52 cm.

76 **Henri de Toulouse-Lautrec,**
*Jane Avril Dancing,*
1891, oil on cardboard,
85.5 × 45 cm.

# Contemporary Life

77 **Gustave Caillebotte**
**(1848-94),**
*Planing the Floor,*
1875, oil on canvas,
102 × 146.5 cm.

78 **Edgar Degas**
**(1834-1917),**
*Women Ironing,*
ca. 1884, oil on canvas,
76 × 81.5 cm.

79 **Edgar Degas,**
*Absinth,*
ca. 1876, oil on canvas,
92 × 68 cm.

Caillebotte and Degas both chose to depict contemporary life, a subject often treated by the naturalist writers of their time. Paintings of workers, such as *Planing the Floor* and *Women Ironing*, do not reflect any particular social statement; the artists real aim was to capture the immediacy of a gesture. Reality was rendered without any artifice or formal composition. In *Absinth*, Degas presents an unforgiving vision of urban solitude. The unusual viewpoints make these scenes from everyday life look like spontaneous images captured in the lends of a camera. Caillebotte and Degas shared an eminently modern and realistic view toward the organization of the pictorial space, in which the figures occupy a space equivalent to the emptiness that surrounds them. C. N.

79

78

# Renoir

81

"If God had not created a woman's neck, I don't know if I would have been a painter." This remark by Renoir reflects his great love of women, particularly those with opulent forms. Around 1883 the painter abandoned his Impressionist approach and fine brushstrokes for a clearly defined style, although he later considered it to be overly harsh. Dissatisfied with his figures that lay flat against the background, he destroyed many of his canvases and returned to a more fluid style, with a lighter palette that included pinks and pearl-whites. He replaced the smooth, interlacing brushstrokes with transparent layers of superimposed light colors, inspired by Rubens' scumbling technique. *The Bathers* and *The Swing* reflect this same desire to meld the figures into the landscape, as if he wanted the drawing to blend into the color. C. N.

80 **Auguste Renoir (1841-1919),**
*Study. Torso, Effect of Sun,*
ca. 1876,
oil on canvas, 81 × 65 cm.

81 **Auguste Renoir,**
*The Swing,*
1876, oil on canvas, 92 × 73 cm.

82 **Auguste Renoir,**
*Women Bathing,*
1918-19, oil on canvas,
110 × 160 cm.

82

# Monet

83

Sometime around 1880, Monet began a lifelong quest to capture the variations of light that changed with the time of day and the seasons. He would work endlessly on single subject. "Every day, I add or I discover something that I had never been able to see before." His first series of paintings of the Rouen Cathedral was created in this way. The shapes gradually dissolved into a diffuse work of fragmented subject matter and pure, thick color; the forms themselves became immaterial.

In his London cityscapes, the architecture, the surface of the Thames River and the fog worked together to form an evanescent vision. Monet painted the water lilies in his Giverny home over and over again, as he tried to capture every possible variation of light and reflection in the water gardens. He remained obsessed with the lilies to the end of his life. C. N.

83 **Claude Monet**
**(1840-1926),**
*The Rouen Cathedral,*
*Main Door*
*and Saint Romain Tower.*
*Morning, Harmony in White,*
1893,
oil on canvas, 106 x 73 cm.

84 **Claude Monet,**
*London, The Parliament.*
*A Gap of Sunlight in the Fog,*
1904,
oil on canvas, 81 x 92 cm.

84

85

**85 Claude Monet,**
*Blue Waterlilies,*
1916-19, oil on canvas,
200 x 200 cm.

# Rodin

Rodin pushed sculpture to
the limits of its
expressive and narrative
capacities. He
particularly wanted to
render the features
of human physiognomy
and postures.
He was even accused
of casting his
own face as a model for
*The Age of Bronze*.
The light sparkles over the
sculpted surfaces of
his marbles and bronzes,
as in his modeled clay
studies. With these works,
Rodin abandoned the
smooth surface treatment
that was in fashion
at the time. When
he met Camille Claudel
in 1883, he recorded
their tumultuous love in
*The Gates of Hell*,

88

86 **Auguste Rodin
(1840-1917),**
*Monument to Balzac,*
1897, plaster model,
275 × 121 × 132 cm.

87 **Auguste Rodin,**
*The Age of Bronze,*
1877, bronze,
178 × 59 × 65.1 cm.

88 **Auguste Rodin,**
*The Gates of Hell,*
1880-1917,
plaster high relief,
625 × 4 × 94 cm.

89 **Camille Claudel
(1864-1943),** *Mature Age,*
1893-1903, bronze,
114 × 163 × 72 cm.

a commission from the
government. Drawing
his inspiration
from Dante's *Hell,* Rodin
concentrated on
the themes favored by the
Romantics: the
human passions.
He created independent
sculptures for each
part of this monumental
work. Although
the *Monument to Balzac*
was commissioned
in 1891, the bronze piece
was not cast until
20 years after the death of
the sculptor. The
extreme simplification of
form in this
sculpture represents a
break with the
declamatory gestures and
the ideal nude
popular at the time. **C. N.**

89

# 1886-1914
# The Reign of the precursors

*Suddenly the pace of art history quickened
and Impressionism, which appeared at the end of a
heroic decade, was bypassed by the more
radical formal research of several independent artists.
Gauguin, Van Gogh and Cézanne became
the great precursors of twentieth-century art.*
**By Thalie Goetz**

91

The year 1886 marked a turning point,
even a rupture, in the history of French painting.
In this year the Impressionists held their last
group show together and new artists began to
question the recent advances in painting. For two
years the neo-Impressionists, inspired in part by
Seurat's *Bathers at Asnières* (Tate Gallery, London), developed their ideas and in 1886 they
formed their own movement at the second
Salon des Indépendants. That same year the
Symbolist manifesto was published. Although it
dealt primarily with poetry and fiction, its spirit
soon extended to the visual arts as well. Indeed,
one of the reasons Paris was the art center of
the world at the turn of the century was due to the
close relationship between writers and painters.
Van Gogh went to Paris with the specific intention of contacting the intellectual effervescence

92

93

of the French capital. It was there that he made friends with Signac, Emile Bernard, Toulouse-Lautrec and Gauguin. Of the major painters, only Cézanne stood apart, as he lived and worked in Aix-en-Provence, in southern France.

Unlike the Impressionists, the neo-Impressionists wanted to rigorously apply the results of optical research, even though they still used similar subjects: seascapes and views of the Seine, scenes from daily life and portraits. As art critic Félix Fénéon pointed out, Seurat innovated by dividing tones into pure colors. "Instead of mixing colors on his palette which, once put on the canvas, would approximate the color of the object being represented, the artist placed brushstrokes that corresponded to the local color of the object, others that corresponded to reflections cast by adjacent objects, and still others representing the complementary colors of the overall light." This seemingly technical reform, based on the scientific writings of Chevreul, in fact led to a complete redefinition of artistic thinking at the end of the century. However, it would be a mistake to think that neo-Impressionism was intended merely as a rigorous application of a scientific theory: Seurat hoped to elicit an emotional response from his visual play of lines and colors.

Shortly after the birth of neo-Impressionism, Jean Moréas signed a manifesto in the September 1886 literary supplement of *Le Figaro*

that signaled the birth of Symbolism. Unlike other movements at the time, no particular mode of expression was preferred over another. In the words of the poet Verlaine, "There are as many symbols as there are Symbolists." Symbolists wanted to give a free reign to ideas; according to one definition, Symbolism was meant "to tell the onlooker something; like poetry, to give him something to think about; or like a piece of music, to transmit an impression." The Symbolists refused the brutal transformations that were taking place around them and idealized the values which they sensed would soon be lost. A number of them, like Moreau, Gauguin and Redon, took refuge in the mystical or imaginary worlds they created.

One of the principle initiators of the movement was Paul Gauguin. He had previously worked in the Impressionist style, taking his inspiration for his portraits and landscapes from Degas and Pissarro. Though he exhibited with the Impressionists from 1879 to 1886, his works attracted little attention. Abandoning the broken brushstrokes of his first, Impressionist period, Gauguin began to use color so subjectively that at times it no longer corresponded to objective reality. To this he added a highly original sense of composition. In the half-length portrait of *The Beautiful Angèle* (96), the figure is separated from the background by a half-circle that recalls a Japanese hair-frame. The Peruvian-looking,

92 **Paul Signac (1863-1935),** *Red Buoy, Saint-Tropez,* 1895, oil on canvas, 81 × 65 cm. After the death of his friend Seurat – whose divisionist technique he continued to defend – Signac traveled to the Midi where he discovered Saint-Tropez and Antibes.

93 **Henri-Edmond Cross (1856-1910),** *The Golden Isles,* 1890-1892, oil on canvas, 60 × 55 cm. While Signac drew the *Red Buoy* with wide brushstrokes and brilliant colors, Cross created a quasi-abstract chromatic study.

94 **Georges Seurat (1859-91),** *Circus,* 1891, oil on canvas, 185.5 × 152.5 cm. *The Circus* was Seurat's last work, left unfinished when he died after a sudden illness. As opposed to most of his paintings, in this work the painter tried to express movement and expression.

anthropomorphic ceramic pieces placed in front of a decorative landscape indicate the symbolic intentions Gauguin wanted to convey in his portrait painting. In the Breton village of Pont-Aven, where he lived and worked in 1888, Gauguin brought to fruition the experiments of the preceding two years. In close collaboration with Emile Bernard, he elaborated the theory of Synthesism or Cloisonnism, which he later developed fully in Tahiti, and which Paul Sérusier was to teach to the Nabis.

In Synthesism, forms are simplified, flat colors are applied over fairly large areas, and traditional Western perspective is replaced by a daring asymmetrical composition reminiscent of Japanese prints. Many artists had been working in Brittany since the 1860s, where they found "nature devoid of any trace of modern life, where Druid, Catholic and feudal ruins are scattered about the countryside like so many loose pages of a forgotten history book." Gauguin, who had spent part of his childhood in Peru, found it "wild and primitive." As he wrote to his friend Schuffenecker, "My wooden shoes make the same dull, powerful sound that I want to create in my paintings."

Tahiti was the last stage in Gauguin's quest for primitive religious sentiment. The paintings done during the last 20 years of his life were devoted to developing Synthesism (*Women of Tahiti*, 115; *Arearea*, 91; *The White Horse*, 117). His interest in native rites led him to create what Octave Mirbeau called in 1891, "a disquieting mixture of barbarian splendor, Catholic liturgy, Hindu dreams, Gothic imagery, and subtle, obscure symbolism."

95

96

97

**95 Paul Gauguin (1848-1903),**
*Les Alyscamps. Arles,*
1888, oil on canvas,
91.5 × 72.5 cm.
Gauguin painted the ancient necropolis of Alyscamps during his trip to Arles to visit van Gogh. The colors seem to be ablaze, threatening the three strangely immobile figures.

**96 Paul Gauguin,**
*The Beautiful Angèle,*
*Madame Satre,*
*innkeeper in Pont-Aven,*
1889, oil on canvas,
92 × 73 cm.
In a description of this work to his brother, Van Gogh wrote that "the women resembles a young cow, but there is something so fresh, and again, so rural, that it is a real pleasure to see."

**97 Paul Gauguin,**
*Breton Peasant Women,*
1894, oil on canvas, 66 × 92.5 cm.
Gauguin, in his search for the simplest possible forms, developed the theories of cloisonnism with Emile Bernard. The scenes and visions of a timeless Brittany satisfied his need for formal primitivism.

**98 Paul Sérusier (1863-1927),**
*The Talsiman, Aven in the*
*Bois-d'Amour, Pont-Aven,*
1888, oil on wood, 27 × 21.5 cm.
Sérusier painted this work under Gauguin's guidance, "a small formless landscape, because synthetically formulated," according to Maurice Denis.

98

100

When Van Gogh arrived in Paris, his first paintings recalled the realistic portraits and country scenes done in his native Holland. He used dark colors in an expressive style. But his style quickly changed as he discovered the latest artistic trends and met other painters at Cormon's studio or at Pere Tanguy's paint shop. From the Impressionists, he learned to use pure, bright colors. With Paul Signac, he tried his hand at neo-Impressionistic landscapes in the suburbs of Paris, but instead of using rigorous technique for its own sake, he put it to decorative use. He was so taken with strong colors and with Japanese prints that he decided to go to Provence, where he thought he would find landscapes similar to those in Japan. Interested by the solutions proposed by Gauguin and Emile Bernard, he became aware of the expressive powers of color. "Things here have so much style," Van Gogh wrote his brother Theo, "and I want my drawing to become more spontaneous, more exaggerated." He did a number of portraits in

In direct response to the aesthetics proned by Gauguin, the Nabi group (from the Hebrew word for prophet) was formed in 1890, shortly after Paul Sérusier painted *The Talisman* (98), a rapidly executed work with a totally free use of colors, done under the supervision of Gauguin, the "Master of Pont-Aven." The Nabis were a kind of congenial brotherhood that included Denis, Sérusier, Bonnard, Vuillard and Ranson, among others. Like Gauguin, they were above all interested in a painter's freedom. "The principal subject," wrote Bonnard towards the end of his life, "is the surface, which has colors and laws that go beyond the objects [painted]." The Nabis as a group were ready to dare anything and had no time for such conventions as traditional perspective, preferring Japanese-style composition instead. What varied was their subject-matter: Denis's mysticism as opposed to Vuillard's intimacy and Bonnard's modern approach (*The Croquet Game*, 122). Like the English pre-Raphaelites, they wanted to bring poetry into daily life. Without exception, they all cried "Walls, give us walls to decorate."

101

Auvers-sur-Oise, including the portrait of Doctor Gachet (90), which he himself called *Apparition*. In the same year, his visionary *Church at Auvers-sur-Oise* (112) took on a tragic, premonitory dimension.

In 1884 Toulouse-Lautrec settled in Montmartre and soon became a passionate chronicler of music halls and brothels. It was there that he slowly built up his "Olympus," which included, among others, the song-writer Aristide Bruant, dancer Jane Avril and singer Yvette Guilbert. He would have remained a mere chronicler had it not been for his sharp eye for psychological traits and the sureness of his drawing. Often painted on pieces of cardboard, his scenes were like snapshots executed with exceptional directness, which he succeeded in transposing to his posters thanks to his use of flat colors and stylized drawing.

During his youth, when he was still a provincial painter with few contacts in Paris, Paul Cézanne produced some highly personal, baroque works that seemed to be remnants of some kind of Romanticism. This period was characterized by

dark colors applied in thick daubs and expressive distortions. Cézanne was briefly attracted to the technical and aesthetic experiments of the Impressionists. Working with Pissarro, he abandoned chiaroscuro as well as the complex subject-matter of his earlier works. By working on his subject directly, he began to use brighter colors, but by 1873, with *House of the Hanged Man* (53), his almost uniform use of a grayish-green and his desire to build a coherent composition herald his mature style. The artist's frequent stays at Jas-du-Bouffan, his home near Aix, helped him along. In *L'Estaque* (64), the parallel brushstrokes, the acccentuated geometric forms and the use of linear perspective all work together to create an intellectual representation of space. Its logic cuts across traditional boundaries; indeed, the portrait of *The Women with a Coffeepot* (120), which is treated like a landscape or a still life, reflects the artist's famous declaration to "treat nature through cylinders, spheres and cones." But color harmony is the point at which rigorous construction and visual emotion meet. In the still-life *Apples and Oranges* (119), there are only a few yellow-orange and

102

103

104

102 **Henri Rousseau
(1844-1910),**
*The Snake Charmer,*
1907, oil on canvas,
169 x 189.5 cm.
The painting was commissioned
by the mother of Robert
Delaunay, the Comtesse de
Rome. This jungle was apparently
inspired by the comtesse's
travel stories and green plants in
her apartment.

103 **Maurice Denis
(1870-1943),**
*Sunlight on the Terrace,*
1890, oil on cardboard,
24 x 20 cm
Maurice Denis invented
the famous formula summarizing
the painter's right to
absolute freedom. "Remember
that a painting… is first
of all a plane covered by colors
arranged in a specific order."

104 **Félix Vallotton
(1865-1925),**
*The Ball,*
1899, oil on cardboard
glued to wood, 48 x 61 cm.
Along with the painter's
technique of using large masses,
this painting presents
a composition similar to the
cinematographic
views of a "traveling" camera.

105

105 **André Derain**
**(1880-1954),**
***Charing Cross Bridge, London,***
ca. 1906, oil on canvas,
81 × 100 cm.
Derain was sent to London
during the winter of 1905 and
spring of 1906 by Vollard
to make a series of views to
compete with those of Monet,
which were exhibited in
the Durand-Ruel gallery in 1904.

106 **Henri Matisse**
**(1869-1954),**
***Luxe, calme et volupté,***
1904, oil on canvas,
98 × 118 cm.
This work is both the completion
of Matisse's experiments
with Signac in 1904 and
the starting point for a subjective
use of color that made Matisse
the leading figure of Fauvism.

gray-green tones, but they are used with such intelligence that they create the relief and the light specific to each object. Though Gauguin, Van Gogh and Cézanne were still considered marginal artists by Establishment critics on the eve of the twentieth century, they had, in fact, laid the foundations for a new approach to painting. For the coming generations, a return to primitivism and to pure colors, as well as a new sense of composition, were to be the order of the day.

The last rooms of the Musée d'Orsay are devoted to Fauvism, which in some way highlights

106

the ambivalence of this short-lived movement. Some of the most vital trends of late nineteenth-century art came together in Fauvism, and the Fauves' preoccupations made it an art form that heralded future trends. Almost all the artists who were known as Fauves had worked in the studio of Gustave Moreau, where they learned about the "necessary richness of color." Furthermore, Van Gogh's use of color was seen as a revelation when his works where shown at the Galerie Bernheim in 1901. To paint his *Luxe, Calme et Volupté* (106), Matisse worked alongside Signac during the summer of 1904. These various experiences set off the dynamics of color which became the basis for the Fauvist movement. Brought together for the first time at the 1905 Salon d'Automne by Matisse, the principal proponents of Fauvism – Derain, Vlaminck, Marquet, and Van Dongen – profoundly disturbed the public and the press by declaring their determination to free painting from its shackles, including naturalistic concerns. They proclaimed that line and color were to reign supreme, an attitude that sent shock waves through decade after decade of the twentieth century.
**Thalie Goetz**

# Seurat

107

According to Fénéon, Seurat's *Nude Models* was "the most ambitious effort of Art Nouveau." Indeed, Seurat created this composition of three nudes just when certain critics, hostile to divisionism, claimed that faces and bodies could not be represented with this technique. The studies for this large painting (now part of the Barnes Foundation) are already the work of a mature artist. Each of the figures refers to a classical prototype: *The Valpinçon Bather* by Ingres and two antique models, *Venus* and *The Thorn Puller*. Furthermore, for the first time, Seurat painted the frame, to create a chromatic transition between the painting and its environment. In *Nude Models*, the painter adhered strictly to his new method: division of color and pointillist brushstrokes. The disappearance of line in favor of modeling can also be seen in his Conté crayon drawings. The silhouettes emerge from a dark mass that vibrates with an infinite variety of grays. C. N.

107 **Georges Seurat,**
**(1859-91),**
*The Black Knot,,*
1882, Conté crayon, 31 x 23 cm.

**Georges Seurat,**
108 *Model in Profile,*
109 *Front View of Model,*
110 *Model from Behind,*
1887, oil on wood, 25 x 16 cm,
Three studies
made for *The Bathers.*

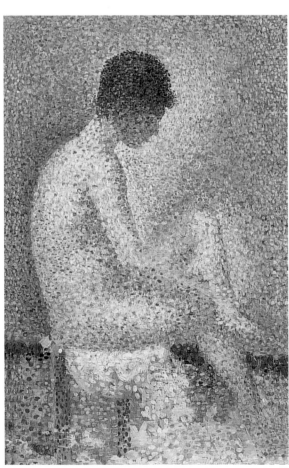

108

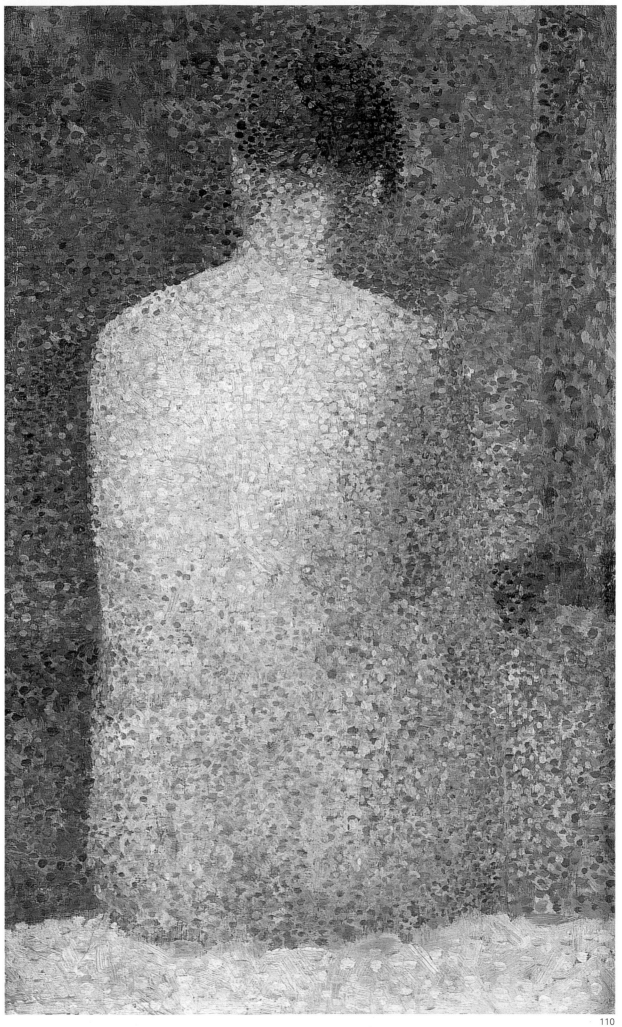

# Van Gogh

111

In 1878 van Gogh lived in the Borinage with Belgian miners. Until 1885, his painting was marked by the influence of this experience, reflected in dark colors and heavy brushwork. In Paris, his brother Theo introduced him to Toulouse-Lautrec, Emile Bernard, Pissarro, Signac and Gauguin, and he discovered the technique of the Impressionists. He added bright color to his palette and his brushstrokes became livelier and more distinct. The artist's personality emerged after he moved to Arles in 1888 and his colors attained an astonishing, unprecedented intensity as he worked in the light of the Midi. While he struggled desperately with illness and a world that rejected him, van Gogh's style became more radical: his brushwork became feverish and tormented, his lines sinuous and his colors exaggerated. **C. N.**

112

111 **Vincent van Gogh (1853-90),**
*Self-Portrait,*
1889, oil on canvas,
65 × 54.5 cm.

112 **Vincent van Gogh,**
*The Church at Auvers-sur-Oise,*
1890, oil on canvas,
94 × 74.5 cm.

113 **Vincent van Gogh,**
*Father Eloi's Farm,*
1890, graphite,
pen and brown ink,
48 × 61 cm.

114 **Vincent van Gogh,**
*Van Gogh's Bedroom*
*at Arles,*
1889, oil on canvas,
57.5 × 74 cm.

113

114

# Gauguin

At the age of 35 Gauguin abandoned a promising career with the Bertin bank to become a painter. He traveled to Martinique in 1887 and made a second trip to Pont-Aven in 1888. Through these travels, he rapidly evolved his style from Impressionism to Synthesism. Gauguin favored the ornamental aspects of drawing and "pure color," independent of reality. In 1891 he traveled to Tahiti and was overwhelmed by the beauty of the Polynesian people and landscapes. He discovered the classical rhythms of Egyptian bas-reliefs, the flat colors of Japanese prints and the luxuriance of tropical colors. He went beyond the purely picturesque aspect of painting and became interested in the forms and concepts of primitive art, along with its religious and magical symbols. Octave Mirbeau defined his polychrome sculptures as part of a "complicated and primitive, light and dark, barbaric and refined" art. C. N.

115

115 **Paul Gauguin (1848-1903),** *Women of Tahiti* or *On the Beach,* 1891, oil on canvas, 69 x 91.5 cm.

116 **Paul Gauguin,** *Be Mysterious,* 1890, bas-relief, painted lime-wood, 73 x 95 cm.

117 **Paul Gauguin,** *The White Horse,* 1898, oil on canvas, 140 x 91.5 cm.

116

# Cézanne

Along with the famous Saint-Victoire Mountain and the bathers, apples were one of Cézanne's favorite subjects. Indeed, still-lifes were ideal supports for his formal research: he could combine the simple shapes of the fruits with the complex surface of drapery in extremely well-planned compositions. These compositions completely overturned traditional perceptions about space. However, the symmetry of the construction and geometric approach to the figures in *The Woman with the Coffeepot* and the five versions of *The Card Players* reflects the artist's desire to simplify his compositions. In the years from 1890 to 1895, his use of colors was fully developed. "When color is exuberant, form is replete," explained Cézanne. C. N.

118 **Paul Cézanne
(1839-1906),**
*The Card Players,*
1890-95, oil on canvas,
47.5 × 57 cm.

119 **Paul Cézanne,**
*Apples and Oranges,*
1895-1900, oil on canvas,
74 × 93 cm.

120 **Paul Cézanne,**
*Woman with a Coffeepot,*
1890-95, oil on canvas,
130.5 × 96.5 cm.

119

# Nabis

121

122

121 **Edouard Vuillard
(1868-1940),** *Public Gardens:
The Conversation,* 213 × 154 cm;
***Nannies,*** 213.5 × 73 cm;
***The Red Umbrella,***
214 × 81 cm, 1894, oil on canvas,
panels for wall decoration.

122 **Pierre Bonnard
(1867-1947),**
***The Croquet Game or
Dusk,***
1892, oil on canvas,
130 × 162.5 cm.

123 **Maurice Denis
(1870-1943),**
*The Muses,*
1893, oil on canvas,
171.5 × 137.5 cm.

124 **Pierre Bonnard,**
*The Dressing Gown,*
ca. 1890,
oil on cloth, 150 × 50 cm.

123

**Bonnard, Vuillard
and Maurice Denis formed
a small group they called
the Nabis, a Hebrew word
that means "prophet."
They wanted painting
to be recognized as a great
decorative art, which was
an important part
of everyday life. As Maurice
Denis explained,
"the Nabis believed that for
every emotion, every
human thought, there
existed a plastic,
decorative equivalent, a
corresponding beauty."
They received numerous
commissions to decorate
private townhouses,
theaters and illustrations
for** *La Revue Blanche.*
**Folding screens were
covered with large areas of
flat colors or with tiny
brushstrokes in
the style of the pointillists.
Every element – from
simple cloisonné
shapes to extravagant floral
designs – were used to
create, in the words of
Baudelaire, this "synthetic
and abridged" art. C. N.**

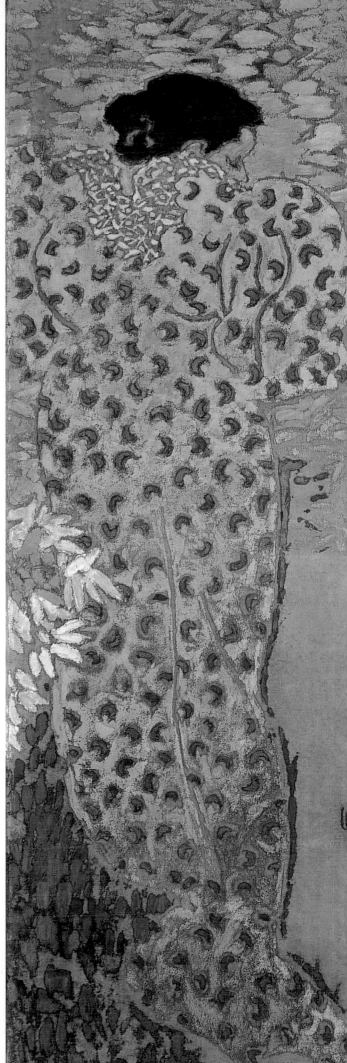

124

# Symbolism

During the last quarter of
the 19th century,
writers and poets reacted
against the positivism that
marked a world
dominated by machines by
joining the Symbolist
movement, a trend that
spread rapidly to the
visual arts and included
several tendencies, one
of which was the
precursor of the English
Pre-Raphaelites, founded
in 1848. It attracted
all sorts of idealists who
had broken with
Realism – the official art
of the Salons – and
Impressionism. The latter
privileged sensations,
while the Symbolists, on
the contrary, were driven
by their imagination
and their dreams. Their
favorite subjects were
drawn from mythology
and the fantastic, and
were marked by anguish,
silence and death. Several
generations of artists
were represented: in
France, they included
Gustave Moreau and
Puvis de Chavannes, then
later, Odilon Redon
and Paul Gauguin. T. G.

125 **Edward Burne-Jones
(1833-98),**
*The Wheel of Fortune,*
1875-83, oil on canvas,
200 × 100 cm.

125

127

126 **Gustave Moreau (1826-98),** *Orpheus,* 1865, oil on wood, 154 x 99.5 cm.

127 **Pierre Puvis de Chavannes (1824-98),** *Young Girls at the Seaside,* 1879, oil on canvas, decorative panel, 205 x 154 cm.

128 **Odilon Redon (1840-1916),** *The Shell,* 1912, pastel, 51 x 57.8 cm.

126

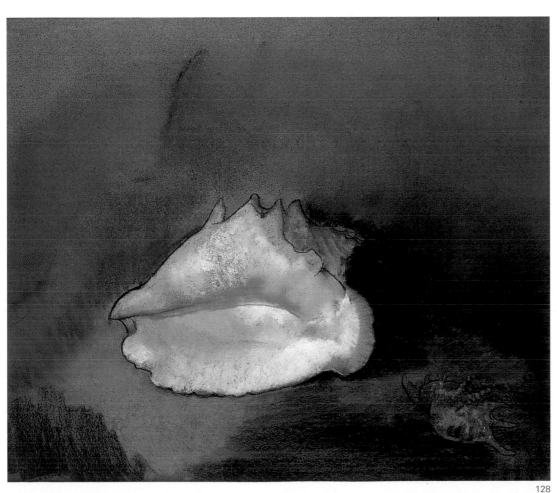

128

# Maillol, Bourdelle, Bernard

Gide, discussing the Salon of 1905, compared the "anxious, gasping and pathetic" work by Rodin to Maillol's *Mediterranean*, a seated, silent woman that "transmits nothing." The massive forms, without the coyness of official art or the expressionism of Rodin, represented beauty in its simplest expression. The fluid and sinuous silhouette of Joseph Bernard's *Water Carrier* also reflects this search to attain harmony and balance. Son of a master stone-cutter, Bernard was one of the first to stress the "life of the material," and favored a smooth surface that he sculpted himself. Bourdelle, a disciple of Rodin, freed himself from his master's influence by developing a more constructed and angular style. His technique contributed to the birth of the Art Deco style. C. N.

129

130

129 **Aristide Maillol,**
**(1861-1944),**
*Desire,*
1905-07, lead,
120 × 115 × 25 cm.

130 **Aristide Maillol**
*Mediterranean,*
1905-27, marble,
110 × 117 × 68 cm.

131 **Joseph Bernard**
**(1866-1931),**
*Water Carrier,*
1912, bronze, 175 × 40 × 52 cm.

131

132 **Emile-Antoine
Bourdelle (1861-1929),**
*Hercules the Bowman,*
1909, gilt bronze,
248 × 247 × 123 cm.

133 **William Morris
(1834-96) and
William-Frend de Morgan,
decorative panel,**
ca. 1876, enameled stoneware,
163.5 x 90.5 cm.
Morris adapted the floral
vocabulary of wallpaper and
furnishing fabric to
architectural ornamentation.
The use of ceramic
panels, cornices and cabochons
spread throughout
Europe in the late 1800s.

134 **Henry Toussaint
(1849-1911),**
*Project to transform the Eiffel
Tower into a Palace
of Electricity and Civil
Engineering for the Universal
Exposition of 1900*
pen, gouache and watercolor,
90 x 114 cm. Eiffel collection.
An "empty chandelier,"
or the "apotheosis of a viaduct
pillar," according to
Huysmans, Eiffel's manifesto was
subjected to a multitude a
proposals – it was to be covered
and/or renovated – before
it achieved a symbolic legitimacy.

# The Designs of prosperity

*The economic upheavals of the century signaled the arrival of a new era for architecture and the decorative arts. In these remodeled cities, bourgeois apartments and their interiors were decorated with an eclecticism created from diverse historical styles. Around 1890, designers adopted the flowing lines and abstract geometry of Art Nouveau. By Nicolas Blondel*

134

**T**he modern city arose in the nineteenth century during the golden age of industrial capitalism. The populations of Paris, London, Berlin and Vienna grew exponentially and architects were called on to design entirely new neighborhoods. To affirm their power and prestige, governments multiplied the symbols of their opulence by constructing buildings that became centers of these new urban entities: law courts, universities, post offices, town halls, barracks, churches, banks and theaters appeared along the main roads of these new areas. Private town houses sprung up at the edge of parks on land divisions created by rich financiers such as Pereire; these mansions reflected the prosperity of the new business class. Zola astutely described this milieu of Paris in his Rougon-Macquart series, particularly *La Curée*.

135

136

This same Paris, redesigned by the prefect Haussmann, also saw the appearance of a new type of bourgeois building, which had several floors and rooms under the eaves for the servants.

What kind of style to use for these constructions? The neo-classicism that began during the Empire with Percier and Fontaine was replaced in the 1830s by a return to styles of the past, a phenomenon that contributed to the eclecticism of the mid-nineteenth century. With the Ecole des beaux-arts, France remained the great guardian of classical tradition and this vision traveled all over the world, to Austria, the United States and even South America. Furthermore, each European country renewed its connection with

its own past: Vienna with the Imperial Baroque; Berlin, a younger city, was marked by the influence of Schinkel and his followers; while London was divided between the neo-Gothic style and a fascination with the neo-Palladian tradition. New centers flourished around 1880: Glasgow, Darmstadt, Munich, Weimar, Brussels and even Nancy, where Art Nouveau architecture developed.

These new buildings, often characterized by fine-quality ornamental sculpture, contained apartments that were richly decorated by craftsmen and furniture-makers, who gave free reign to their imaginations. Industrial progress meant that it was possible to make better objects for less money. The Universal Exposition of 1851 in London allowed the entire world to see the best – as well as the worst – objects in industrial arts design in Western civilization. Neo-classicism, which provided objects inspired from antiquity throughout all of Napoleonic Europe, was waning. New industrial processes had distributed and devalued the mythological gods and victories that characterized neo-classicism. The neo-Gothic and neo-Renaissance styles recreated a repertory of forms that often overlapped. Other styles appeared in the following decades, adding an exotic note to these mixtures of styles. These included Japonism, Orientalism and even neo-Greek and neo-Prehistoric styles.

Manufacturers in the fields of porcelain, silver, ceramics, and copper and brassware competed to present new shapes to the largest possible public. Decorative bronze-makers such as Barbedienne used new techniques to making smaller versions of sculptures to create lamps and clocks from works made by fashionable sculptors like Carrier-Belleuse. The Christofle company began to use electroplating, an industrial process that

138

considerably lowered the manufacturing costs of silver-plating. This intersection of history and industry delighted the new bourgeois class, which was reassured by tried-and-true repertories, and hesitant toward the artists who were creating simpler, more audacious works.

In the last decades of the century, new designers tired of the overly opulent forms of eclecticism, and a preference developed throughout all of Europe for pre-industrial age craftsmanship. This return to simpler, "well-crafted" forms started early on in England with A. Welby Pugin and the Arts & Crafts movement in the late 1840s, and in France with Viollet-le-Duc, a historian and theorist of medieval art. The

137

139

140

supposed austerity of the medieval age had a strong influence on new works until Art Nouveau appeared in 1900. Japan was also a reference in this return to more structural simplicity. Modern Japanese creations strongly influenced western designers, who felt they had discovered an artistic enclave on the other side of the world that had somehow escaped the damaging effects of modernism.

These revival movements led to the creation of a new, spare style around 1890. It developed in Glasgow, where Charles Rennie Mackintosh had developed a geometric floral style that included subtle Symbolist elements. This sophisticated simplicity spread quickly through the many decorative arts exhibitions held throughout Europe. The Glasgow School influenced artists in Vienna (Otto Wagner and his students Josef Hoffman and Koloman Moser), Darmstadt (Joseph Ollbrich), Munich and Brussels (Henry van de Velde). New industrial techniques contributed to the realization of these designs that ushered in modern design. Otto Wagner and Adolf Loos recreated the

traditional bistro chair by using the bentwood technique developed by the Thonet company in Austria. Similarly, the industrial production of square-section lengths of wood meant that chairs could be mass-produced.

The influence of the Arts & Crafts movement was transformed into a veritable floral art in Brussels, Nancy and Paris. Bypassing the constraints of classical ornamentation, they were able to imitate nature without falling into the geometric abstraction that appeared with Art Deco at the end of World War I. Van de Velde glorified the flowing curve – inspired from interlacing Celtic designs – and transmitted it to Berlin and to Wiemar. Even Victor Horta in Brussels adopted it enthusiastically in a bourgeois society ready to accept this new style. Nancy, which since the annexation of Alsace in 1870 had become an influential center of industrial design, adopted Art Nouveau as a modern manifesto. Victor Gallé produced masterpieces in glass, inspired by the study of the flora and fauna of his natal Lorrain. He was less at ease

139 **Alphonse Nicolas Crépinet (1826-92),**
*Project for the new Paris Opera,*
1861, lead pencil and watercolor,
50.6 × 68.9 cm.
The construction of the Opera was the great project of the Second Empire. This project, excessive in its Haussmannian uniformity, was abandoned for the more sensational conception of urban space proposed by Garnier.

140 **Eugène Grasset (1841-1917),**
*Work by Industry and Commerce Enriches Humanity,*
ca. 1900, charcoal and wash on paper, 146.7 × 129.5 cm. Central section of a stained glass commissioned by the Paris Chamber of Commerce for the conference room; this glass is still in place at 21, rue Notre-Dame-des-Victoires.

141 **Auguste-Joseph Magne (1816-85),**
*Vaudeville Theater, elevation drawing of the front,*
1870, lead pencil, watercolor, pen and black ink with gouache and gold highlights, 81.4 × 50 cm. Haussmann conceived of the city as a monumental theater, where the overall perspective was more important than the talents of the architect. The Magne theater fits serenely into the surrounding order and is only noticeable from the decorative elements symbolizing Comedy.

141

142

143

**142 Charles,**
*Bordeaux Bridge,*
photograph with oil-paint
highlights by Petraud,
17 × 75 cm. Eiffel collection.
Less spectacular than
the viaducts by Eiffel,
the bridge by Charles is a good
illustration of the
industrial design of cast-iron
architecture, by using
elements prefabricated on the
mining sites.

**143 Maurice Boille
(1883-1966),**
*Entrance to the Métro,*
Godebœuf competition, 1910,
pencil and watercolor,
68.5 × 104 cm.
The increasing transportation
methods resulted in
the creation of new types of
buildings (stations and bridges).
In Paris, the métro
entrances were also included
in the urban design project
(which included
fountains, kiosks and urinals).

**144 Hector Guimard
(1867-1942),**
**design for middle of stone
balcony,**
iron, 35 × 93.5 cm.
As the forerunner of Art
Nouveau in France, Guimard
conceived of living spaces
as an integral unit in which line
and function, architecture
and furniture were designed
according to an ideal
of modernity and well-being.

**145 Carlo Bugatti
(1856-1940),**
**one of a pair of "Cobra"
chairs ,**
ca. 1902, mahogaony and
painted vellum,
114 × 45.3 × 50 cm.
Father of the famous
automobile manufacturer,
the cabinet-maker
Carlo Bugatti incorporated a
diverse number of
exotic shapes and materials in
objects for the rich,
cosmopolitan pre-war society.

**146 Emile Gallé
(1846-1904),**
**cornet,**
1900, blown crystal with
particles of metal,
gold, platinum, etched glass and
glass pearls, 49.6 cm high.
This vase, treated
as a cameo through
a multitude of technical
processes – often
carefully guarded by the master
glassmakers – was
inspired from *The Trojans*, an
opera by Berlioz.

146

144

with furniture design, a domain he yielded to
Majorelle, who brilliantly combined gilt bronze
and mahogany. The great master of Art Nouveau,
however, was Hector Guimard, a talented drafts-
man and designer, who continued to design
Art Nouveau objects until the outbreak of
World War I. He was able to create both popular designs – the Paris Métro entrances, for example – and elitist interiors for wealthy clients.

There is no "period room" in the Musée d'Orsay, and the paintings, sculpture and objects are
exhibited separately. Yet several rooms have
been reconstructed, such as Alexandre Charpentier's dining room (151) and Jean Dampt's
drawing room. The first reveals the opulence of
a bourgeois family that transformed the dining
room into a celebration of family intimacy. The
second reflects the interior of a great collector,
the Comtesse Martine de Béhague, who commissioned works from the greatest artists of
her time for her private townhouse in Fau-
bourg-Saint-Germain, where she received the
finest figures in the artistic and literary world.
**Nicolas Blondel**

145

# Decorative eclecticism

148

147

147 **Charles Guillaume
Diehl (1811-ca. 1885),**
with the collaboration of
**Jean Brandely
and Emmanuel Fremiet,
medal cabinet,**
ca. 1867, cedar, walnut,
ebony, ivory, bronze and copper,
238 x 151 x 60 cm.

148 **Paul Christofle
(1838-1907),**
with the collaboration of
**Mathurin Moreau,**
*Vase Depicting the Education
of Achilles,*
Salon of 1861,
oil on canvas, 69 x 124 cm.

149

150

The decorative arts did not escape the spirit of opulence and eclecticism that seized the entire society. During the Second Empire, people loved historical styles, but only when they were revised and corrected: this led to a neo-Greek, neo-Renaissance and even neo-Louis XIV style, among others. With the help of sculptors and architects, cabinet-makers were able to produce remarkable works for the world's fairs in Paris, such as a Merovingian-style medal cabinet by Diehl and Frémiet. Other leading establishments, such as Christofle or Barbedienne, created such marvels. Only the Emperor or the richest families could afford such magnificent objects, but thanks to the recent marriage of art and industry, even bourgeois families could acquire quality pieces designed by artists and produced industrially. C. A.

149 **Henri-Auguste Fourdinois** (active from 1850 to 1878),
*Athena*,
sculpted oak and walnut, ebony marquetry, red marble, gilt bronze, enamel, overall dimensions of door: 480 x 280 cm.

150 **Charles Lepec** (1830-85),
*Clémence Isaure*,
1865, enamel painted on copper, 180.3 x 111.3 cm.

# Art nouveau

Regardless what it was called – Modern Style, Arte Joven, Jugendstil or Art Nouveau – the new art that developed during the last 25 years of the nineteenth century took on a decidedly international dimension, in keeping with its ambitions. Following the ideas of such dissidents as Viollet-le-Duc in France and Ruskin in Great Britain, its proponents refused to accept the academic or naturalistic works that had dominated the art scene for several decades. They favored a return to the study of nature. They were interested in introducing beauty into everyday life and making it accessible to all classes of society. Two main tendencies stand out among this flourishing of ideas: one based on floral inspiration, embodied in France by the School of Nancy; and the other a rationalistic trend, represented by the Glasgow School and the Wiener Werkstätte. T. G.

152

151

151 **Alexandre Charpentier (1856-1909), dining room for the villa of banker Adrien Bénard in Champrosay,** ca. 1900, mahogany, oak, poplar, gilt bronze, fountain and stoneware tiles by Alexandre Bigot, 346 × 1055 × 621 cm.

152 **Hector Guimard (1867-1942), armchair,** 1898-99, American walnut, 116 × 68 × 52 cm.

153 **Koloman Moser
(1868-1918),** *Archangel,*
**detail of** *Paradise,*
1904, drawing for the stained
glass of the Saint-Leopold Church,
the Steinhof sanatorium, Vienna,
distemper on paper, overall
dimensions: 415 × 774 cm.

154 **Charles-Rennie
Mackintosh
(1868-1928), desk,**
ca. 1904, colored glass,
lead and brass,
121.9 × 81.3 × 41.9 cm.

155 **Joseph Hoffmann
(1870-1956),
Jacob and Joseph Kohn
company,**
*Reclining armchair,*
ca. 1908, bent beechwood,
plywood, mahogany-color
varnish, brass, 110 × 62 × 82 cm.

153

154

155

# Photography a new spirit for the image

*Photography was one of the most revolutionary discoveries of the nineteenth century and it occupies an important place in the Musée d'Orsay. The collection, which consists of several thousand images, retraces the epic adventures of the early years of photography: the revelation of the technical progress, its rivalry with painting and the search for its own artistic identity. By Hervé Vanel*

157

**B**y creating a photography department, the Musée d'Orsay wanted to bring this mode of expression back from the fringes of art history where it had long been classified. The ambiguous status of photography began as early as August 19, 1839, when François Arago revealed Daguerre's discovery to the Académie des sciences. The irrefutable truth of the photographic image was enough to convince him of its usefulness in such diverse scientific fields as zoology, astronomy and archeology. Yet it was a painter, Paul Delaroche, who convinced Arago that the "unimaginably delicate finish" of this representation of reality would contribute to the "progress" of art.

Some ten years after this revelation, while Daguerre's process was developing both technically and commercially, Eugène Delacroix

156 **Robert Demachy (1859-1936),**
*Landscape,*
ca. 1904, gum dichromate print,
21.2 x 15.8 cm.
Robert Demachy, a banker, took
up photography as a
rich amateur before it became his
true vocation.
He was one of the major figures
of French pictorialism.

157 **Charles-Victor Hugo (1826-71),**
*The Dicq,*
*Breakwater at Jersey,*
1853, print on salted paper
from albumin glass negative,
16.1 x 19.8 cm.
Print from the album
*Victor Hugo Photographer.*
When Charles-Victor Hugo
traveled to Jersey
to visit his exiled father, Victor,
the greatest poet
of the nineteenth century,
he carried a camera
in his suitcase to pass the time.

158

**158 Pierre Bonnard
(1867-1947),**
*Model in the Artist's Studio,*
ca. 1912, silver print,
8.8 x 5.9 cm.
This is a corner of the studio at
22, rue de Tourlaque, where
Bonnard worked from 1911 to
his death. As in many of
his works, the painters used the
mirror to admirable effect.

**159 Etienne Carjat
(1828-1906),**
*Portrait of Eugène Delacroix,*
1861-62, albumin print
from a collodion glass negative,
25.4 x 18.6 cm.
Delacroix, the leading
figure of the Romantic school
– who claimed he was
not romantic – was elected to
the Academy in 1857; here,
Carjac captured the mood of an
impenetrable commander.

**160 Félix Tournachon
known as Nadar
(1820-1910),**
*Sarah Bernardt,*
ca. 1860, print on
salted paper from glass negative,
21.4 x 17.2 cm.
Many visitors passed through
Nadar's studio, including
Sarah Bernhardt, only 16 when
this portrait was taken.

159

160

deigned to express a certain tolerance for this
new way of "correcting the eye's errors"; yet
this response only veiled his contempt for the
weak spirit of painters who were already taken
in by this "despairing perfection." Indeed,
Daguerre's experiments became a societal
phenomenon. In 1859 Baudelaire grasped the
immensity of the disaster with acuity and furor.
"Because the photographic industry became the
refuge for failed painters . . . this overwhelming
popularity not only seemed to be blind and
stupid; it was also colored with vengeance."

Baudelaire, like Delacroix and Sainte-Beuve
and in general, all the intellectual elite of Paris,
were nonetheless frequent visitors to the
photographic studio opened by Nadar in 1853.
They were all fascinated by the portraits made
by Nadar and Etienne Carjat. This fascination,
which exists to this day, was probably due to the
fact that these photographers did not consider
the mathematical objectivity of the process as
the essential element to reproducing a likeness.
Indeed, although the technique of photography
was available to everyone, Nadar warned
that "the sentiment of light" and "the moral
intelligence" of the photographed subject was
not something that could be taught.
This same viewpoint also held true for landscape

161 **Edward Steichen
(1879-1973),**
*Self-Portrait with his Wife,*
1903, print on glycerin-coated
paper, 22.3 x 25 cm.
With Steichen, the American
*Photo-Secession*
movement established a real link
with modern art.
The psychological tension of this
self-portrait confirms
photography's new identity as
an art form.

photography. Today, the technical mastery displayed by Henri Le Secq, Victor Regnault and especially Gustave Le Gray in landscape photography is still impressive. According to Françoise Heilbrun, it is no exaggeration to compare their masterpieces with the fresco work of the thirteenth century, "wherein the problem of paint drying too fast . . . meant that fresco painters developed an extraordinary confidence in their own drawing." Indeed, the variations in light intensity that struck different parts of a landscape forced the photographers to multiply the length of the exposures, or, as in the seascapes by Le Gray from 1856-57, to combine two different negatives to freeze the movements of the clouds, the sea and the mist in a single image. Yet our view of these photographers known as "primitives" must also be seen in relation to what a painter such as Turner

163

was producing some ten years earlier with *Rain, Steam, Speed*. The fundamental immobility of the photographic image was not particularly well suited to the modern efforts to depict the world in motion. This drawback was challenged by the "pictorialists" in Europe and United States, particularly Robert Demachy, Frank Eugène and Clarence Husdon White; they were the first to use soft-focus photography and defended the single print at the expense of the reproducibility inherent in their medium.

In conjunction with these esthetic arguments, the appearance of the instantaneous image advanced the analysis of the decomposition of movement studied by Marey and Muybridge. This led to some vague scientistic theories, such as the systematic classification of the "characteristic attitudes and movements of lunatics."

The history of early photography is both rich and complex, and the interest shown by the Musée d'Orsay allows us the privilege of seeing the medium within the artistic context it which it developed – somewhere between the troubling *Olympia* by Manet and the "pastry" goddesses by Cabanel. **Hervé Vanel**

162

162 **Charles Aubry (worked in the 1860s),** *Anemones,*
1864-65, print on albumin paper from a collodion glass negative, 37 × 27.2 cm.
Studies of flowers, leaves and fruits by photographers were used by painters and designer working in the industrial arts, particularly for fabric designs.

163 **Gustave Le Gray (1820-84),** *Steam, Le Havre,*
1856, print on albumin paper from a collodion glass negative, 32 × 41.3 cm.
Just like landscape painters such as Boudin, Le Gray composed subtle seascapes that depicted the play of clouds, rolling waves and moving boats.

164 **Frank Eugène (1865-1936),** *Adam and Eve,*
1910, photogravure from original negative, 18 × 12.8 cm.
Franck Eugène, a promoter of soft focus and an ardent supporter of "artistic photography," used varied techniques to make photography a substitute for painting.

# Orsay, practical information

**Musée d'Orsay,**
62 rue de Lille, 75343 Paris cedex 07
Tel: 40 49 48 14.

**Main entrance**
1, rue de Bellechasse
**Entrance for temporary exhibitions**
place Henry-de-Montherlant
(quai Anatole-France).

Bus: 24, 63, 68, 69, 73, 83, 84, 94
Métro: line 12, Solférino station.
RER: line C, Musée d'Orsay station.
Taxis: rue de Solférino
and quai Anatole-France
Parking garages:
Deligny, Louvre, Montalembert.

**Informations**
General information
(recorded announcement): 45 49 11 11
Information booth:
40 49 48 48 and 40 49 49 94
Minitel: 3615 Orsay.

**Opening hours:**
The museum is open to the public,
Tuesday, Wednesday,
Friday and Saturday 10am to 6pm;
Thursday 10am to 9:45pm;
Sunday 9am to 6pm. Closed Monday.
Last admission 5:30pm
(9:15pm on Thursday)
Rooms start to close at 5:30pm
(9:15 on Thursday).

**Services**
Cloakrooms, telephones, mailbox
and exchange bureau,
loan of strollers, wheelchairs.

**Restaurant on the middle level**
Open 11:30am to 2:30pm and Thursday
7 to 9:15pm; tea room open
3:30 to 5:30pm (except Thursday).

**Rooftop café (upper level)**
Open 10am to 5pm, Thursday to 9pm.
Tel: 45 49 47 03.

**Bookshop and card shop:**
Entrance from place Henri-de-
Montherlant (quai Anatole France) or
from the museum, tel: 40 49 47 22.

**Boutique:**
Entrance from the main square.
Open 9:30am to 6:30pm,
Thursday to 9:30pm. Tel: 40 49 49 99.

**Guided visits**
Overall visit, by theme or by artist,
visit of a temporary exhibit: 1.5 hours;
"A work to see": 1 hour; presentation
of a dossier-exhibit: 1 hour.

Groups (maximum 30 people):
Tuesday to Saturday, 9am to 2:30 pm,
Thursday
9am to 2:30pm and 6 to 7:30pm.
Reservations required
with or without museum guide:
school groups, tel: 45 49 45 46,
adults, tel: 45 49 16 15.

Headset rental:
French, English, Italian, Spanish, German and Japanese.

### Classes and conferences
The Musée d'Orsay and the Ecole du Louvre organize cultural history classes reserved to students of the school and "Carte Blanche" holders. Series of conferences and debates are held, depending on the museum exhibitions, on Saturday 11am to 12:30pm. Free admission by invitation available on the day of the conference between 10 and 11am at the "individual" information booth.

### Concerts
Concerts are held in the auditorium and sometimes in the museum reception room. Concerts at 12:30pm, 6:45pm and the evening. Information and reservations, tel: 40 49 47 17 ou 40 49 48 90.

### Cinema
The Musée d'Orsay offers a discovery of the nineteenth century through films, documentaries and short films. Programmed two Fridays per months at 12:30pm, they provide a new look at art, artists, history or literature. Free entrance, reservations not required.

### Children's activities
Organized visits available for children 5 to 10 years old (not in a group), Wednesdays at 2:30pm and during school vacations. Information and prior reservations at the museum, at the Espace des Jeunes, level -1 or tel: 40 49 49 76.

### Groups
The activities are described in the "Centre de Loisirs" brochure and in the "Activités pédagogiques" brochure for school groups. These documents are available at the information booths of the museum or sent on request by calling 40 49 49 76.

### Cycles and day visits
The cycles and day visits, for Musée d'Orsay Carte Blanche holders, take place either in the Musée d'Orsay or in several museums. They are presented by lecturers from the national museums. Day visits: 10:30am to 12:30pm and 2 to 4pm. Cycles: Three 1.5 hour visits.

### The Musée d'Orsay Carte Blanche
The Musée d'Orsay Carte Blanche, individual membership card, is valid one year from the purchase date. The Musée d'Orsay Carte Blanche, group membership, is valid from January 1 to December 31 of the current year. Group rates are available for groups of at least ten members. The Carte Blanche offers many advantages: reduced or free entrance to exhibits, visits, conferences, concerts, reductions at the bookshop and restaurant. Information at the information booths or by calling 40 49 48 65 or 40 49 48 72

### Société des Amis du Musée d'Orsay
Tel: 40 49 48 34.

166

165 **The head of Mercury overlooking the glass roof of the museum.**
© Stéphane Couturier/Archipress.

166 **The museum restaurant on the middle level.**

# order of the visit

ground floor
upper level
middle level

# ground floor

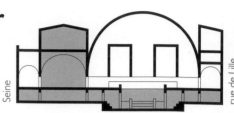

Seine
rue de Lille

## access

 up

 down

 escalator

 staircase

 lift for
the handicapped

## departments

 sculpture

 painting

 architecture

 decorative arts

 the " Dossiers "
of the Musée d'Orsay

## services

 toilets

 cloakroom
for individuals

 cloakroom
for groups

 telephone

 post

 change

 audioguide

reception desk

## room numbers

**59** the numbers marked on
this map are also indicated on the
room signs of the museum

---

### sculpture
- central aisle:
  sculpture 1840-1875,
  Carpeaux
- **2** Barye
- **4** Daumier

### painting
- **1** Ingres and followers
- **2** Delacroix, Chassériau
- **3** history paintings and
  portraits 1850-1880
- **4** Daumier
- **5** Chauchard collection
- **6** Millet, Rousseau,
  Corot
- **7** Courbet
- **11** Puvis de Chavannes
- **12** Gustave Moreau
- **13** Degas before 1870
- **14** Manet before 1870
- **15** Fantin-Latour
- **16** open-air painting
- **17** pastels
- **18** Monet, Bazille, Renoir
  before 1870
- **19** Personnaz collection
- **20** Mollard collection
- **21** pastels
- **22** realism
- **23** orientalism

### decorative arts
- **9** decorative arts,
- **10** 1850-1880

### architecture
pavillon amont
(alteration works
under way):
- **24** architecture
- **25** and furniture
- **26** from Viollet-le-Duc
- **27** to Frank Lloyd
- **28** Wright

### M'O Dossiers
- **8** Dossier 1
- " Opera " room:
  Dossier 2

# upper level

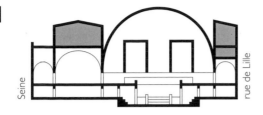

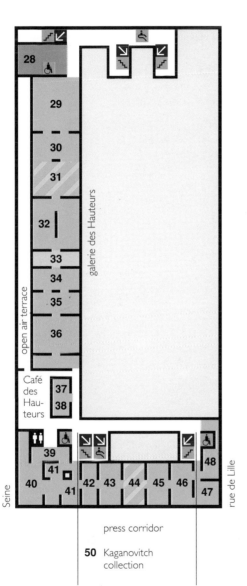

# middle level

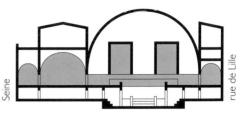

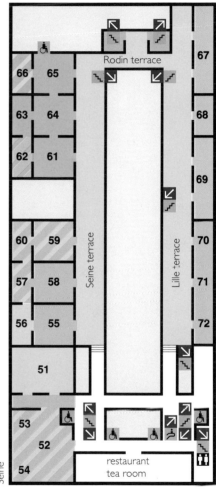

**Les hors série Beaux Arts magazine sont édités par Beaux Arts S. A. Président-directeur général :** Charles-Henri Flammarion. **Directeur de la publication :** Jean-Christophe Delpierre. **Directeur de la rédaction :** Nicolas Chaudun. **Secrétaire générale de la rédaction :** Pascale Bertrand. **Maquettiste :** Claire Luxey. **Secrétariat de rédaction :** Isabelle Arson. **Secrétariat de rédaction pour les versions étrangères :** Isabelle Gilloots. **Version anglaise :** Lisa Davidson. **Version espagnole :** Marie Cordoba. **Version italienne :** Federica Zucchi. **Version allemande :** Karen Rudolph. **Version japonaise :** Kodama Kikuko. **Version russe :** Natacha Iakaitis. **Commentaires d'œuvres :** Philippe Dufour, Thalie Goetz, Michèle Haddad, Manuel Jover, Caroline Larroche et Caroline Naphegyi.

**Beaux Arts magazine**, tour Montparnasse, 33, avenue du Maine, 75755 Paris Cedex 15. Tél : 01 45 38 30 00. Fax : 01 45 38 30 01. RCS Paris B 404 332 942. **Commission paritaire** 65094. **Dépôt légal :** juin 1997. **Directeur de la fabrication :** Alain Alliez, assisté de Nathalie Laudat. **Responsable des ventes :** Isabelle Canals.(tél : 01 45 38 30 60, fax : 01 45 38 30 61).

Imprimé en Italie par Mariogros S. p. a. © Beaux Arts Magazine.

Nous remercions Corinne Guichard pour son aide.